THE ME
I COULDN'T SEE

A JOURNEY INTO AUTHENTICITY

ALISON ASTARA

ISBN 978-1-957943-51-0 (paperback)
ISBN 978-1-957943-73-2 (hardcover)
ISBN 978-1-957943-52-7 (digital)

Rushmore Press LLC
1 800 460 9188
www.rushmorepress.com

Printed in the United States of America

TABLE OF CONTENTS

"A Successful Man
is one who can lay a firm foundation with
the bricks others have thrown at him."

--David Brinkley

"The biggest wake-up call in life is realizing you are
so programmed by your own emotions and society
that you don't know who you really are."

--Alison Astara

ABOUT THE BOOK

This book is a fictional work based on a true story of one woman's journey into authenticity. The names and places in the book are purely fictional and are not meant to identify any particular person or place.

The purpose of this book is to encourage people, especially women, that they are much greater than they ever dreamed possible; much more powerful than any trial or obstacle. By tapping into the authentic you, you can create miracles and change your life the way you want it to be. It doesn't mean you won't experience pain. Pain is a part of life. But you will learn which kinds of experiences and people work for you in life and which ones don't, and you can make decisions that strengthen and support yourself rather than self-sabotage.

This book is dedicated to anyone who has ever felt like a victim. You have a choice to liberate yourself. Let the stories in this book show you a way to find your authentic power and purpose of your life, and introduce you to "The Me I Couldn't See". What you will find there is more beautiful than you ever dreamed possible!

INTRODUCTORY OVERVIEW

"Each man's life represents a road toward himself."

- Herman Hesse

I f anyone would have said to me 20 years ago that I would be writing a book about how to change your life, I would have laughed. My life had been cycling in negative patterns for years. Finally, the cycling finished its course, I crashed and burned, and I found **The Me I Couldn't See.**

As I look back on my life, it has been full of experiences that took me on a journey to discover who I really am--not the little girl that grew up the daughter of an alcoholic father; not the younger sister who was pushed forward because she was the "extrovert"; not the teenager who sought love through boys who were willing to say they loved her; not the "A" student who graduated at 16 because she was way beyond her years intellectually; not the young wife who needed so desperately to have a baby so she could love and be loved; not the divorcee who kept on hoping that one of these guys she married would really understand who she was and just simply love her. None of these experiences defined who I was. They were simply experiences that I designed to find myself... the **authentic** me.

Many of my first 35 years were full of traumatic experiences, but I gave birth to three wonderful girls whom I deeply loved. It was because of them I had a reason to live and I never gave up. I know that sounds dramatic, but my life was dramatic! I have been through situations that most people only have nightmares about. If you believe in karma, I definitely had lots to resolve. I married several times, setting myself up by selecting relationships that couldn't achieve authentic love or emotional intimacy. I have had to face death on many levels, including an illness that diagnosed me as having six months to live and then a massive head injury from a fall that caused me to die and return in an instant.

After many tragic experiences, I felt I had started over so many times that I didn't know if I had the energy to do it again. But, in spite of the drama and the trauma, at a certain point in my life I sold everything I owned at a garage sale (which tells you how well things were going) and started over. I had $200 to my name and what was in my van. I left my 12-year old daughter with my Mom until I could find a new job in another state. I knew it was time to completely break a life pattern and begin anew. I was tired and I was sick, but I had developed many skills in marketing, medicine, and entertainment. I was determined to be successful and prepare a place to live for my youngest daughter and me that was drama-free.

I am thankful that I had a true friend. That's the kind you can call after not seeing them for 25 years and they say, "Come stay with me. I'll help". Stephanie helped me get back on my feet and encouraged me that she had made just as many mistakes as me (which at the time was very hard for me to believe). I'll never forget her faith, kindness and generosity; but the most valuable thing she did was to reflect back to me all my good qualities.

Within a few weeks, I secured a job in radio broadcasting as a sales person. It didn't pay much of a salary, but the potential for commissions was great. That first year I made more money than I ever had in my life, and it skyrocketed from there. I was able to put all my performing arts and marketing skills to use, and found that my intuitive abilities helped my clients and made me a top seller at the station. That was the next phase (and most important) of my journey into "The Me I

Couldn't See". I would learn much about myself over the next 20 years, and would face some of the toughest challenges anyone can possibly face in this lifetime; grief, humiliation, betrayal, grave illness and a COMPLETE RESURRECTION! All of the endings brought new beginnings, and for that I am grateful.

I want to share my story with you because I think it might help you in some way. Perhaps it might even save you from some of the darkness I went through. So, if you are at a place in your life where nothing is working, guess what? You're right on track! Now, just look inside your heart. **The Me I Couldn't See** is waiting there to meet you.

Alison Astara

CHAPTER 1

FROM HEAVEN TO EARTH INTO THE THREE DIMENSIONAL BOX

"Heaven means to be one with Creator."

- Confucius

Weighing in at six pounds, I was the fifth child of my clan. I joined a quartet of siblings—three brothers and a sister. I loved my new family, and was ready for lots of cuddling, sleeping and eating.

My father was a dashingly handsome man with a 1940s movie star's persona. With a medium build and sun-tanned Norwegian skin, he was strikingly attractive, with penetratingly large, dark eyes, and hair that was immaculately trimmed to draw attention to his Clark Gable moustache. I adored him, and he adored me. He loved all his children, especially when they were little, but his two little girls always seemed to warm his heart with delight. When he was clear-headed, he cherished us as precious treasures to be handled with loving care.

Unfortunately, the dark side of my father's ego identity did not quite live up to his external persona. While seemingly confident and debonair, internally he suffered from a continual lack of confidence and an intense sense of failure. Feeling powerless to live up to his own potential, he drank away his pain, and our family life was scarred by the ravages of alcoholism. I spent years overcoming the damage done to my psyche as a result of this disease and my misunderstandings and misperceptions about myself and love because of it.

Alcohol numbed my father's sense of responsibility, especially where money and parenting were concerned. His interest in raising children waned as soon as we were out of diapers, so my mother was left to raise us with inadequate support emotionally and materially.

Mom was of hearty stock. She was raised on acreage in the country, and her mother was the queen of making lemonade from whatever life brought forth, most of which were lemons during the Great Depression. My grandmother had suffered greatly her entire life, and yet could always find the time for a hug, a smile, and little love. She taught my Mom how to survive in the worst of conditions, and that is exactly what my Mom did most of her adult life while having to endure the pitfalls of an alcoholic husband. She survived. She learned how to raise five children on her own. With the burden of financial scarcity, she also went to work to support us and make sure we had clothes and shoes.

Mom was often embittered by the fact that my father was irresponsible, and the fighting over money and alcohol was a constant happening in our home. Yet, while my Mom tried to focus on doing things that were positive, she exhibited anger and resentment over my father's actions. She didn't realize that we could also sense and feel her pain and desperation. She worked hard not to say negative things to us about our father, and she thought that by not talking about his alcoholism, she would spare us from it. She never really understood, until we became adults and it was vocalized, that we knew and felt everything that was going on, dramatically. While she was doing what she thought would bring us hope for a future that wouldn't be limited, she allowed herself to fall victim to her own resentment and anger.

Both my parents had survived the great depression, and as a result, suffered throughout their lives over their perceptions of not having enough to subsist. It is interesting now to reflect back and see how they both had the same survival instincts, and yet they manifested them in opposite ways. My mother would choose to ration things, focusing on pennies and self-sacrifice. My Dad lived with a "take it now, 'cause it won't be there tomorrow" attitude. As I grew up, their different responses to their environment had a penetrating and confusing effect on me, and also created a devastating imbalance in their relationship. The lack of money or resources and escapism vs. responsibility seemed to be their recurring life themes.

When I look back on the women in the 40's and 50s, they were all dealt a very difficult life. Many women of this era were unhappy and didn't have the ability to earn enough to support themselves independently. They lived in fear that they wouldn't be able to feed and clothe their children if they left their marriages. As a result, they stayed in their relationships and took emotional and physical abuse, limiting themselves and their ability to find the truth about themselves and Creator. Women have had a particularly difficult time through the centuries. The world was (and still is) full of imbalance, judgment and power and control by the dysfunctional masculine. It has not been true until now that we are capable of going beyond it. Women, it's finally our time! The time for the feminine aspect of Creator is here to be recognized and accepted by patriarchal hierarchies of religion. If they can't accept the feminine aspect of Creator, they cannot receive understanding and compassion. They are missing out on a very critical part of Creator's nature.

When I was an infant, my mother received a rare invitation to see a movie with a friend and take a break from her duties as a housewife and mother of five. With little money, this gift was one she treasured and needed, and she left all five of us in the care of our father, which was a rare occurrence.

Unfortunately, my father took my mother's absence as an opportunity to drink, and he continued to drink throughout the evening until he was quite drunk and out of touch with his rational self. I began to cry for attention. My father came to me, but in his drunken stupor, he snatched me up and placed me in a box and closed the flaps before he passed out cold.

In the darkness, I was filled with terror, and I cried louder and louder. I cried and cried, but no one came. For the first time in my short human existence, I felt the oppressive limitation of three-dimensional reality, trapped and abandoned.

"Where did everybody go? Don't they know I'm scared and hungry? Did they throw me away? I thought they loved me! My cries bounced off the sides of the box and back into my body. I screamed and kicked against the sides of the box, but no one came. I felt completely alone and in utter terror and panic, separated from love and light for the first time in my life. It was so dark and black in there. Where were the angels? Where was Creator? It felt as if even they had abandoned me.

After what seemed like hours, my mother picked me up out of the box. My little body had cried so hard and for so long that I was almost limp, soaked with sweat, my heart still pounding wildly. She held me close, kissing my cheeks, trying to console me, and I slowly recovered my sense of safety in her arms. Then her warmth and nurturing, protective side gave way to fury. With me still in her arms, she began to verbally lash out at my father. She didn't know that every angry word went right into me too.

Had I done something wrong? Don't they love me anymore? Am I not good enough? Why was I thrown out like garbage? Feeling fear and rage, feeling that I wasn't good enough to be loved, and being scared for my life became indelibly inked in my subconscious mind and trapped in the memory within every cell in my body. It was the beginning of subconscious patterns that would play out in very dramatic ways, including assault, rape and near death much later in life.

CHAPTER 2

LEARNING ABOUT HUMANITY

"Someday, after mastering the winds, the waves, the tides and gravity, we shall harness for God the energies of love, and then, for a second time in the history of the world, man will have discovered fire."

- Pierre Teilhard de Chardin

A few years later, as a toddler, I experienced the shift from my authentic connection to the limitations of the human realm even more graphically. It began with a tent, a tricycle and lots of confusion about gravity.

I was a tiny little one, so I often stood in the palm of my Dad's hand as a toddler, as he thrust me up into the air with my arms outstretched. In these times, I experienced the familiar feeling that I was flying. I had perfect balance and no fear. It was wonderful and exhilarating.

One day, my three brothers had set up a tent in the back yard, and had gone fishing for the day, expecting to come home and camp out in the back yard. I was at home with Mom, and began riding my tricycle in the backyard. As I looked over at the tent, it dawned on me that I could ride my bike right up the side of the tent to the top, and then I could fly. It made perfect sense to me that the tent presented another opportunity to be in the sky, feeling free and flying high. I peddled as hard as I could toward the side of the tent, and to my complete dismay, ripped a gaping hole right through the side, leaving me stunned that I was inside rather than on top. What happened? Why couldn't I ride up the side? Why was I here instead of at the top? The rules of physical reality seemed wrong in this place.

I had trouble understanding what just happened. Heartbroken, I dejectedly went to tell my Mom, and she was angry with me, which confused me even more. When we picked up my brothers, they all got angry too, and treated me like the first-class brat who destroyed their camping trip. I was heartbroken.

Didn't they know I was supposed to be able to fly? Didn't they know my angelic connections were so strong, that this was devastating for me? I was left with a feeling of horror that things weren't like they were supposed to be, and unfortunately, those innocent and naïve perspectives continued into many years of misunderstanding the truth of physical law versus cosmic law. But as a toddler, all I could think was "I don't belong here! Nobody sees me."

CHAPTER 3

KINDERGARTEN: MEET THE BULLY

"Bullying, to me, starts very small around the kindergarten age where the first thing we learn is to call each other names. Something so small can be so long lasting in someone's life."

- Shane Koyczan

My first day of school. I was 4 years old. My Mom told me later they accepted me because my birthday was close to the cutoff date. She knew I was very advanced for most kids, and admittedly, I would have been bored stiff at home another year! I was bright, creative, and I loved playing and expressing myself. At least I did until I met Alex.

Alex was all boy. He came to school with his shoes untied (I mean really… he didn't know how to tie his shoes at 5 years old?) and a snotty nose and hair that never seemed to lay down flat. And he was LOUD! I mean you couldn't get a word in edgewise because he was always yelling or war whooping or something. I found him too hard to be around, so I instinctively avoided him. The problem was that I seemed to have some kind of internal magnet that drew him in no matter how hard I tried to hide.

One day Alex said he wanted to hold my hand. I said, "No, Alex. I don't want to. You're too loud." But that didn't stop him. He grabbed my hand anyway, and I tried harder and harder to pull it away. I finally broke free, but it caused me to fall down on the asphalt playground and hit my head. I think I was out for a second, but when I came to nobody was around me. Alex, of course, had run away scared. The rest of the kids were all much too busy playing on the monkey bars and playing hopscotch to notice me.

At first I felt sad, but then I grew angry. How dare him! He had no right to make me fall. I told him, "No!" So, I got back on my feet and went to tell the teacher.

Mrs. Golden didn't seem too worried about me. I told her what Alex had done and that I had hit my head, but she told me to shake it off, that I was ok, and I should go back on the playground and play. She had work to do.

Well I wasn't ok. And she wasn't going to do a thing about it! I was very confused. Why didn't she believe me? I told her I hit my head! Didn't she know it hurt? Why wasn't she going after Alex to give him a spanking?

It was my first lesson in injustice. Boys could get away with just about anything and girls aren't always believed. Note to self: Be careful. People won't believe you even though you are telling the truth!

CHAPTER 4

FINDING CREATOR IN RELIGION

"Even if a man spends his life staring at shadows, he will still know where the sun is."

- John H.D. Lucy

When I was just 7 years old, I asked my parents, who weren't religious at all, to take me to church. I remember how they looked at me sideways, but my Dad, who had been raised in the country and attended church weekly as a young boy, said if I wanted to go I should go. So, I would dress up, put on my hat and white gloves, and Mom or Dad would drop me off and pick me up.

I learned many valuable lessons from Sunday School and worship service. I sang from my heart and meant every word of the hymns, and still get goose bumps when I sing Holy, Holy, Holy. I could sometimes see, hear and feel Jesus, the Angels and Creator. My inner spiritual life was still somewhat connected, and I reached for it even though I didn't have adult guidance. I can remember begging my Mom to come with me to church. And she would, on occasion, but she felt very out of place and uncomfortable. She couldn't relax at all.

Sadly, no one in the church saw me. I was just another kid. I brought my dime to add to the collection plate. On the day I was baptized, the elders asked me if I had been visited by a deacon. I hadn't. They asked me if I understood what baptism meant. I said I did. For me at 7 years old, it was simply dedicating myself to Creator in my heart and asking for purification. It was symbolic. I realize now that I could probably have taught the elders and deacons a thing or two about the truth of baptism. Bottom line, they baptized me and never followed up. I was a little plant that was left outside in the elements to shrivel up alone.

It was painful for me not to be recognized in church. I thought I might give Sunday School a try, so I went across the lot to my age group. There the teacher read the story of Solomon and the two women with the dead baby. They both claimed it was their baby, but wise old Solomon said to cut the baby in half and give half to each mother. I was mortified! But then the teacher went on to explain. Solomon knew that the real mother would never want the baby cut in half—even if the baby was dead. Her love would never permit it. So, Solomon waited until one of the women begged not to have the baby cut in half, relinquishing the baby to the other woman. Her compassion toward the child told Solomon in his heart that this woman was the real mother. He ordered the dead child to be given to the true mother and told her to weep and go bury her child in peace.

I was awestruck at a young age at how wise Solomon was. It was then that I began praying to have the wisdom of Solomon. That's what I wanted the most! Wisdom! I didn't want knowledge---you could get that from a book. I didn't want wealth—it paled in comparison to having insight into people so that you could do the right things in life. No, wisdom was the most important quality to have in life, and I knew it at 7 years old!

CHAPTER 5

TERROR IN THE HOUSE!

"Children's emotional security is affected by the relationship between the parents -- not just the child's relationship to the parent."

- E. Mark Cummings, Ph.D.

It was Saturday. My brothers were down the street playing baseball with the neighbors. My sister and I were the only kids home, alone with Mom and Dad, who had subsequently gotten into a full-on fist-to-cuffs.

I remember my sister and I hiding in our bedroom because the screaming was getting louder and louder. We didn't want to get in the middle of them, but then we heard them in a full-on brawl, I ran down the hallway only to find them wrestling each other to the ground in the bathroom. By this time, my Mom was underneath my Dad, and she was fighting to get him off her. Of course, it was the most common fight theme---his drinking. As she fought bitterly, I yelled at them to please stop. Just then I heard my Mom push my Dad's fingers back and I heard them break. Pop! Snap! He yelled in pain, and I could feel the pain in my body. I was so traumatized I ran outside and down the street screaming for help, running as hard and fast as my little legs would carry me. I had to reach my brothers. I was met by a neighbor who came running to help, but I didn't know him very well and wasn't about to stop my furious pace to explain, especially to a stranger. No, I had to reach my brothers! They would know what to do.

They saw me coming toward them screaming and sobbing and ran to meet me. The two oldest went to the house to break up the fight and told the youngest brother to keep me there and calm me down. The neighbors were my Mom and Dad's friends, so they took me inside and tried to console me and get my mind off things. They could see my absolute terror.

I don't remember much about going home. I don't remember my sister and what she did or where she was. I just know that I had gone through a shockingly traumatic event, and I didn't know how to cope with it.

The only thing I could come up was to vow to myself that I would never fight with my husband or in front of my children. Hmmm. A 7-year old's vow that would hold me hostage to my own fear much later in life.

CHAPTER 6

LEARNING COMPASSION AND SHAME

"No one is useless in the world who lightens the burdens of another."

- Charles Dickens

I was in 5th Grade and was in a gifted class. This class was a split 5th and 6th classroom. I was a straight "A" student; the epitome of the perfect little girl. I got most of my self-esteem from doing well in school, although my parents never seemed to care much. I would beg them to go to open house night to see my work, but they would usually just pat me on the head and say they knew I was doing wonderful work. It was rare that they ever went, and as I look back, I realize that it was probably because of my Dad's alcoholism. Mom never really knew if he would be sober or not. We all lived from day to day wondering what the night would bring. I lived in constant fear that my friends would find out that my Dad was an alcoholic. It isn't any way to live, constantly waiting for the other shoe to drop.

Because I learned so quickly, the teacher often put me next to students who struggled. This was usually ok by me, except when he put me next to Scottie. Scottie was probably twice my size, a brute of a kid, who was always sweaty from playing kick ball and who was dumb as a rock. But Scottie taught me a big lesson. Even though he was loud outside and harsh with others, when I helped him with kindness, he responded with gentleness and kindness right back. It seemed to open my heart in ways I didn't know were possible.

It wasn't long before I learned that when I showed compassion, even to the most obnoxious fools, they usually backed off and showed a sweet side. I decided that I would work at that the rest of my life, instead of judging a book by its cover. Only one problem. I became so conditioned to giving to everyone else that I didn't leave anything for myself. That was a lesson that I would have to face head on much later in life. But I am still grateful for the lesson Scottie taught me. It truly is a good thing to show compassion and kindness whenever you can.

My Dad's alcoholism continued to be an issue at home, and I lived in constant fear that people would find out and I would be embarrassed and humiliated. A fellow classmate's Dad was an alcoholic too. I knew he was an alcoholic because he worked for my Dad, and often came to my home to drink with my father. She invited me to her birthday party, along with several other girls in our class. I don't know what came over me. Perhaps it was my own insecurity from my own father's alcoholism, but I told the other girls I wouldn't go because her Dad was an alcoholic. For someone who lived in fear of being found out herself, I had betrayed someone in the same situation.

She found me at school and gave me a tongue lashing that I deserved. She cried. I was so ashamed of myself I cried too. I had humiliated us both with my own selfishness.

I vowed I would never hurt anyone like that again. I still feel the sting when I think about it. It was very cruel of me. To this day, I look back on that event with a sad heart, but I owned it and asked her forgiveness, which was all I could do. It would take me years to forgive myself. After all, I was supposed to be perfect. I was a good girl.

CHAPTER 7

OSCAR THE MONKEY

"Some people talk to animals. Not many listen though. That's the problem."

- A.A. Milne

Not long after 5ᵗʰ Grade my brother gave my sister and me a monkey for Christmas. His name was Oscar. He was a squirrel monkey, a cute little guy that jumped and swung around in his cage. The problem was that he wasn't domesticated. He was wild and needed to be trained.

My sister and I thought he was cute, but we were scared to death of him. He would do wild and crazy things like poop and then throw it against the wall. It was very gross because he lived in our room, and I was a neatnik with a nose for miles. I was constantly cleaning. But as I think about Oscar and his antics, I think about lessons in fear and power and control.

My Dad would get half gassed and then decide Oscar needed a bath. He would put on leather gloves and grab Oscar from the cage. Oscar would always bite my Dad's hands to try to get free, and it would draw blood, biting through my Dad's thick leather gloves. Inevitably, because of my Dad's pain, Oscar would break free and would be running crazy around the house, up the curtains, knocking things off counters and shelves, and ALWAYS hitting the glass coffee pot that sat on the stove, causing it to crash to the ground sending coffee, grounds and glass all over the floor and while he frantically jumped around the kitchen. It was chaos! Pandemonium! Just like you see in the movies! It was comical and scary all at the same time.

Of course, my inebriated father ran around the house trying to catch Oscar, and he always did, finally, after a long-winded chase. And by that time, he was hopping mad and wasn't very kind to Oscar.

Then we got to peek at him as he washed Oscar in the sink. Oscar would continue to bite through the gloves and the blood would run down my Dad's arms. It scared me. I couldn't understand as my Dad cursed him and held him tighter. It all seemed very wrong on both sides. I think my Dad and Oscar were scared of each other and were in a power struggle of the worst kind.

Once, after one of the chaotic episodes, my Dad put Oscar on a leash and tied him outside to our volleyball pole to run and play. Then he proceeded to call a friend so they could drink and laugh about Oscar together.

I'll never forget the two of these grown men getting totally wasted and going outside to taunt Oscar. Oscar would run around the post, much faster than they, and eventually jumped up on the men, spraying them with poop. It was all I could do to keep from laughing. "They got what they deserved, I thought." It was rather comical to see how nature plays out negative energies and karma shows up immediately.

The cursing and the chase around the volleyball pole was quite a bit of comedy, but shameful as well. If they hadn't been drunk, neither of these men would have attempted to "tame" the beast. Perhaps they should have thought about taming the beast within themselves.

CHAPTER 8

THE BIRTHDAY PARTY FROM HELL

"Since self-esteem is based most importantly on the amount of respectful, accepting and concerned treatment from significant others, it is logical to assume that the inconsistency of the presence of these conditions in an alcoholic home would negatively influence one's ability to feel good about him or herself."

- Janet Geringer Woititz

Around age 9 or 10, it was important to have your friends attend your birthday party. It was considered a "must" for your self-esteem. I mean, we needed friends at that age to help us know we were loved and accepted.

Mom created a nice party for me with a Chinese theme, where we sat on a large mat on the floor, had little straw coolie hats, and she had even made me a red Chinese jacket and black pants. It was an adorable outfit, and very creative! No one had a party just like mine! We even had Chinese bobble-head dolls and paper lanterns and umbrellas in our drinks as decorations!

The week before, my Dad, who had been on quite a drinking binge, had asked me one evening after dinner what I wanted for my birthday. I felt it was time to speak from my heart. I said, "Daddy, the best present you could get me is to be here for my birthday and be sober." He immediately discounted what I said and pressed on about what gift he could buy me. I didn't cave in. "All I want is for you to be here for my birthday and not drink. That would make me very happy; it would be the best present in the world."

My big day arrived, and my friends showed up and were excited about the theme of the party. Mom was there serving tea and fortune cookies and providing games for us to play. Then I heard my Dad's truck pull up outside. I jumped to the window and peeked through the curtains. He was so drunk that he fell out of the truck and had to crawl up the lawn on his hands and knees. I went into panic! I didn't want anyone to see my Daddy this way! I yelled to everyone we needed to go in my room.

My Mom picked up on my panic and saw what was going on and immediately called my brothers to come get my Dad out of there. They did, and my Dad was not allowed in the house; my brothers hauled him away. But I was so distraught, so panicked, that I don't even remember the rest of my beautiful birthday party. All I could think was "He doesn't love me enough to show up sober. If he did love me, he wouldn't do this to me."

I was heartbroken. I must not be good enough or Daddy would stop drinking. Why didn't he love me? Why couldn't he just stop drinking for one day? Was that so hard?

CHAPTER 9

MIDDLE SCHOOL CHEERLEADER

"Accomplishments don't erase shame, hatred, cruelty, silence, ignorance, discrimination, low self-esteem or immorality. It covers it up, with a creative version of pride and ego."

- Shannon L. Alder

Seventh grade. Wow, I was moving on up! There seems to be such a sense of being all grown up as one enters middle school. The jump into the teenage years is wrought with emotional questioning, seeking individuation from our parents, and the beginning of figuring out our sexuality. Phew! It's a whirlwind that no one is ready for, and I was no different.

I was lucky to be in the district that had just built a new middle school, even though I didn't live in the wealthy neighborhood. My friends and I were excited about going to a very new, upscale school, which was a far cry from our tiny grammar school in the old district.

It seemed ominous. The classrooms and the campus seemed more like a college to me than a middle school. I liked that. I liked the feeling that I was getting to go to the best school in town, and although it was all new, the school was new too, so we were all newbies!

It wasn't too long until we had auditions for cheerleading squad. Mind you, I had no idea what that was about, except to scream from the sidelines and kick up your heels. My family was never much into sports, so I hadn't grown up watching football like so many families had. Still, it sounded like a pretty cool thing to do. Maybe I could be popular! Wow. That sounded exciting. So, I auditioned. I had been dancing and singing since age 4 and was very coordinated, so I was a natural. Of course, I made the squad.

Our uniforms were pleated white skirts (not too short, mind you) and sweatshirts with the school logo. Not very exciting, but it would do. At least we had pom poms!

Then I found out that our job was to scream and croon on the sidelines for the boys' sports teams. Why weren't we doing anything for girl's teams, I wondered? I guess there just wasn't as many girl's teams as boy's teams. Anyway, it didn't take me long to realize that this game was all about attracting boys and "going steady". Hmmmm. I was insecure enough that I needed that attention, but secure enough that I didn't want to be the "cute cheerleader" who went with the not so bright jock! I wanted someone with half a brain.

I got pretty tired of the game, and never did fall for a football player or any sports player for that matter. It just wasn't my niche. Instead, I spent my extra time doing theater after school at the local community center. That's where most of my friends were since 5th grade, and that is where I could express myself safely through the arts. Things at home were pretty rough, and theater gave me an opportunity to become other people through acting. That allowed me to express all kinds of emotions that I couldn't express honestly and openly in my own life.

The Cheerleading career was short-lived. I decided it wasn't important in 8th grade. And besides, by that time I had attracted in one of the bad boys of 8th grade, so who needed a jock! Why I picked a "bad boy" was a lesson I still needed to sort out and would for many years to come. At that young age, I think it was just because he was popular and my friends thought he was cute. If they wanted him, he must be good, so I followed the crowd, even though he wasn't a football player! He was nice enough and carried my books home from school. It was like the first kiss relationship; but it never went any further. We were still just kids, mostly trying to discover who we were.

CHAPTER 10

MY "CARRIE" EXPERIENCE

"You can be the moon and still be jealous of the stars."

- Gary Allan

High school was long awaited. I was a lovely young lady with quite a brain and was put into advanced classes because of it. I was college prep all the way. The only thing I struggled with was math. My sister, who had preceded me by a year, was a math whiz. Her algebra teacher found the same last name and moved me from a regular math class into his advanced class. I begged him not to put me in his class, explaining that math was my worst subject. He refused. It was one of the hardest classes I ever took. He was belittling to students who couldn't get it quickly and made off-color remarks about the way we dressed and looked. He thought it was funny. None of the girls in his class, especially me, thought there was anything funny about it.

Because I was so geared to continue in theater, I auditioned for the high school musical and got the lead playing Reno Sweeney in the musical, "Anything Goes".

I had no relationships in the theater department at the high school. After all, it was my first year there. The juniors and seniors were livid that the leading role was given to a freshman, and they did everything they could to make my life miserable. One of the teachers was also new that year, and she could see how I was being treated, so she took me under her wing. What was weird was that the teachers seemed divided as well. The two men who were leading the acting and music seemed to have a "club" with the juniors and seniors, and they completely pushed the woman teacher who helped me out of their "clique". It was like her and me against them and the seniors! To this day I still don't understand it. It got worse as rehearsals went on. I kept to myself and it was perceived as arrogant by my peers. It was really only self-preservation. I was there to act, not to be in "the club". I disliked members of "the club" who thought they deserved my role, and I disliked being treated like I had a disease. I kept telling myself that the jealousy would eventually give way to acceptance, but it didn't. Closer to production time my picture was posted on the music department bulletin boards with pins sticking through the eyes. Voodoo dolls began appearing with my name on them with pins sticking through them and ropes around their necks. It was sooooo creepy that it made me scared. But the more it happened, even though my heart was breaking, the more I was determined to be the best I could be. I took the attitude of, "Screw you".

The week before opening, I was asked to contribute money to the teachers' gifts to be presented at the cast party. I asked what was planned for the teacher that helped me. They laughed and said, "Absolutely nothing." It broke my heart that because of me she wouldn't be honored, so I refused to contribute and decided no way would I be going to the cast party given by "the club".

On opening night I received a standing ovation, and my own theater friends saw to it that I was presented with several bouquets of flowers each and every night. It made "the club" furious, especially when I received a telegram of congratulations delivered at curtain call. I was reveling in my success, and enjoyed the attention for the hard work and trials I had been through, but it was short lived.

Now it was time for the cast party. I wouldn't go and had my Mom pick me up and take me home. She called my brothers to let them know of my success and two of them showed up at the house to congratulate me. Upon their entrance, one of my brothers told me there was a big box of flowers on the porch and he assumed they were for me! My Mom asked him to bring them in, and both of us thought they were from him. But we were both in for a big shock.

The box contained freshly caught shark, cut open with blood and guts filling the box. When I opened it, I screamed and threw the box, spilling shark and blood everywhere. I was hysterical. My brothers cleaned it up quickly and my Mom took me into my room where I proceeded to get completely paranoid that "the club" was after me. I wasn't safe! My Mom talked to me and got to me realize that I would be ok. My brothers went back to the porch and found a card that had fallen off the box after it had been placed on the porch. It said, "from the cast and crew".

My brothers went to the cast party and were met with policemen who had been prewarned that they may show up to "crash" the party. They were handcuffed and told if they didn't leave they would be jailed. It was a nightmare. They only wanted to protect and avenge their little sister, but they couldn't. One young man stood up and told the police what the cast had done and that he didn't agree with how they had treated me. He said I didn't deserve it, and neither did my brothers. After his courageous statement, the police let my brothers go. Thank God for someone who was honest!

There was a meeting with the school teachers and the principal about the incident. It seems the teachers connected to "the club" knew what the kids were planning and didn't stop it. Can you imagine? And the darkness grew even darker when the only action taken by the administration was to ask for the resignation of the teacher who had supported me! It was a complete farce.

The rest of my high school years I would be taunted by people in the cast and even the math teacher who refused to let me out of his class. He insulted me continuously saying I had been type-cast, inferring that the character I was playing (a fallen evangelist) was who I was. The battle between light and dark was being played out in my own life. It was definitely karmic, but to this day I can't imagine what kind of jealousy in others and what kind of energy in me would draw in such darkness. It would be the first of a number of experiences with dark forces throughout my adult life. This was just a precursor!

Because I had nothing to keep me at school, and because my grades and my pride were too strong, dropping out wasn't an option. I decided the way to beat them all was to get straight A's and graduate early. I did. A full year early. I never attended any dances, games or events. I never had a junior prom. I kept my nose in a book and all I could think about was getting out of there. In retrospect, I think it probably would have been better to have changed schools, but who knows. As a result of that incident, I stopped doing theater and I stopped hanging around with friends my age. I began dating older men, thinking I might find protection and love.

I still hadn't found The Me I Couldn't See, and was looking for love outside myself in all the wrong places. I couldn't find safety in my peer group so I resorted to older men. Was it because I was trying to find the love of my father in men?

CHAPTER 11

IF YOU CAN'T BEAT 'EM, JOIN 'EM

"Those who follow the crowd usually get lost in it."

- Anonymous

After high school I was on my own, running with an older crowd (I was 17 and my friends were 25+) and doing all the things that twenty-somethings do. It was sex, drugs and rock and roll for quite a while, as I tried to avoid the pain in my own heart. It was as if I had made a choice to do everything everyone else did so I could somehow "fit in". But in reality, I never did. I was just a lost soul trying to find her way.

I dated my 35-year old boss and he left his wife for me. It was a very confusing time. For him, I had become the sex toy he could get to do just about anything. For me it would be a rude awakening when I understood that was all it really was; lust so powerful that he couldn't stay married and play with the young girl, so he separated to have his fantasy.

I'm glad to say that he ended up eventually going back to his wife, and I had decided he wasn't right for me. Besides, I had to look at myself in the mirror and ask myself if I really wanted to be a homewrecker. I didn't. And I didn't want to be a sex toy either, but somehow that was all I kept attracting in. I wondered why someone who wanted to get married and have a baby and live happily ever after kept finding lustful men who wanted a toy. Lustful men were plentiful. And somehow them wanting me sexually made me think I was loved. I really had no clue. I just kept giving myself up to be used and abused. It was a pattern I would repeat for many years until I met "The Me I Couldn't See".

CHAPTER 12

MARRYING MY DAD

"Women who grow up with meaningful, comfortable, conversational relationships with their dads make better choices in who they date, sleep with, and marry."

- Dr. Linda Nielsen

Although my Dad was an alcoholic, he had his wonderful qualities. I could talk to him and he would listen. He taught me how to sing and we sang harmonies together. He used to tap dance in the kitchen, which I always enjoyed. He didn't seem to care about what people thought and would skip down the street with me like a kid. He loved to cook and create. My Dad, even though he was concrete contractor, was an artist, which is why he was probably so good with a trowel. He was sensitive. He always rooted for the underdog. He cared about people less fortunate, and he LOVED BABIES.

Unfortunately, he had never overcome his own trauma of being told he would never amount to anything by his father, and he took to drinking to blind himself to his own pain. The Army didn't do much to help, either. During the war it was commonplace for men to drink like fish and smoke like fiends, and my Dad was no different. The conditioning about women being less than men was also prevalent in my Dad's upbringing. My Mom told stories about his father openly grabbing women's private parts and joking about it. Women in those days seemed to be toys for men to play with and own. They weren't treated as equals.

When I married my first husband, I married my Dad. He was from the Midwest and was a house painter. He loved to drink and play spoons, just like they did in the Midwestern towns. He was easy going. He was kind. He was the kind of guy I wanted to have kids with.

One day on a check-up at the doctor, I was told I was pregnant. I really had no idea. My period was late, but that wasn't unusual for me. It wasn't planned, but I was elated. The doctor told sent me home with pregnancy vitamins and I couldn't wait to tell my husband.

It wasn't the loving conversation I had expected. Instead of being happy, he began yelling out me and accusing me of getting pregnant on purpose without consulting him. He was angry, and all I could do was sob. Who was this man? If he really loved me, wouldn't he be happy I was having his child, even though neither of us expected it? I was reliving the pain of rejection all over again from the deepest parts of me. I sobbed for days, and his attitude didn't change. I was so distraught I couldn't eat or sleep. About a week after the announcement, he came home and said he was sorry to be so mean and he would get used to the idea. I was cold. That night, I miscarried.

That miscarriage was so full of painful emotions that I never got over it. I ended up having an affair and then left my husband. The guy I had the affair with didn't matter. It was just someone else in the moment who might accept me as I am. The bond of marriage was shattered for me when he refused his own child and rejected me as someone who had betrayed him.

In some ways, I married my Dad; the Midwesterner who worked construction and liked music and fun. But the one quality he didn't have that my Dad had was love for babies. And I was crazy about them. His reaction to having a child ended the relationship for me right then and there. I heard much later in life that he remarried but never had children. Go figure. I guess it was part of his journey NOT to have children. Not so with me. I would go on to have three.

CHAPTER 13

MARRYING THE MOB

"You don't attract narcissists because there is something wrong with you. You attract narcissists because so much is right with you"

- Lauren Matthias

I wasn't even 21 and I had been through a divorce. I took to drinking and doing some of the drugs of the early 70s… experimenting with marijuana and LSD. I found that on LSD I was completely free. Nothing scared me. I could see only angels and feel music like it was within me. I understood what the likes of Timothy Leary and others at the Esalen Institute talked about as using it for mind expansion. I was tapping into very high frequencies. I was lucky. I experimented but never had any bad trips, until the last. The last trip I ever took I could see demons. They were like monkeys on my back. I didn't flip out and was calm and secure enough to know that the drug had tapped into a dark reality and I needed to ride it out. I did so, gracefully. And I never took drugs or smoked marijuana again. It only took once!

During that time, I was introduced to a man who was known around town as "The Horse", most likely because he was a bookee who took bets on the horses. He worked as a bartender. He was bold. He was intelligent, and he loved an adventure. Of course he did! He always lived on the edge of the law.

We used to party together, but after dating for some time and moving in together, we decided it was time to have a child. I tried desperately to get pregnant. The day finally came, and we were ecstatic. It was time to get married. You can tell this was a time where marriage wasn't a prerequisite!

We planned a simple wedding at our apartment and he invited a few friends from the bar and his little brother, who had mental and emotional problems. The wedding was nice until the two brothers decided it was time to go on the rampage. They tore the apartment building apart. They were drunk and obnoxious. I was stunned. My new husband spent the night with his mental brother instead of his wife, drinking and carousing and taking drugs until the next day. We were immediately given an eviction notice. One day being married and my whole life was in shambles!

We found another apartment and tried to create a home for our child. I would learn, though, that mental illness and bizarre behavior would run in the family. He would get his other daughter from a prior relationship for the weekend and then he would leave and go on a binge, leaving me to watch the kids. Even though I loved the little girl, it made me resentful. It was hell.

During the pregnancy, I vomited daily, sometimes three or four times. The day our daughter was born I was so sick that I pulled her up out of the birth canal I vomited so hard. The birth was difficult and the cord was wrapped around her neck. We took it slow. I had a natural birth—only oxygen, to ensure that the baby would be okay. She weighed in at 5lbs 14oz, and she was strong. She lost a lot of water weight, but they let me take her home at 5lbs 3 oz because she was holding her head up and looking around in her bassinet. She was amazing.

When she was 8 months old my motherly intuition told me she had a urinary tract infection. I took her to the doctor, who told me that it was very rare for babies. But upon investigation, she had a very serious infection. And upon lab work, we discovered she had a third kidney that was attached to her other kidney on her right side. The tube from the bad kidney (the one that was infected) bypassed the bladder and blocked the urethra. The doctors weren't sure if she would be able to live through a surgery at her young age, and decided to wait until she was a little older. She had to have the bad kidney removed, even though it may mean losing both kidneys on that side or possible death!

Those were the toughest months of my life. My little baby, whom I loved with all my heart, had to be tied down and have her little side cut open and a kidney removed.

I began bargaining with God. Was it because I had done bad things? Was it because I had taken drugs? I hadn't taken any for some time before getting pregnant, but I still questioned if I was to blame. Why did things like this always happen to me?

It was a difficult time at home, too. Money was very tight, so The Horse picked up more shifts as a bartender and began courting the union officials for a job. He taught me how to take his bookee bets so for awhile I became a bookee. I was so naïve I really didn't know that I could be busted for it! I just loved him and wanted to help. It seemed harmless enough to me.

The day of the surgery came when she was 13 months old. I was sick with worry, fear and lack of sleep. She came through the surgery fine, and then it was about recovery. I would spend many days and nights at the hospital, reading to her, singing to her and soothing her. I couldn't pick her up because she was tied down with stitches from her naval to her back with tubes coming out for drainage. No mother ever feels more vulnerable than when their baby is in medical distress. I was praying constantly in gratitude, giving thanks that our little girl was alive and well.

I felt like we had come through that together and that the rest of our lives would be a piece of cake. I pictured The Horse and I sitting on the porch rocking in our rockers in our old age. I finally felt fulfilled.

He got the job as a business agent for the union, and he began working day and night. I stayed at home taking care of our little one until she was 4. Then on my birthday, I got a call... from his girlfriend.

Suffice it to say that the affair had been going on for some time. I was blindsided. He had been living a completely double life. He even had purchased a race horse I knew nothing about.

It wasn't long before I filed for divorce. He wouldn't break things off with her, so I had no choice but to move on. His karma would catch up with him years later and he would die with almost nothing. No wife. His ex-wife cleaned him out, and he was very sick from all the drinking and drugs. I look back now and see how I had lived in a bubble. I chose to see only what I wanted to see. I believed everything he told me rather than focusing on what was really going on. I felt like a stupid little girl. But I could hold my head high that I had lived in integrity and move on without regret. It's just that the moving on part was getting harder. And now my sexuality had been challenged. He left me for another woman... a bartender. And I was a cookie-baking Mom.

I concluded that I wasn't sexy enough. I wasn't good enough to keep someone like this adventurous man who couldn't be tied down. I had given him my best, and it wasn't enough. After that little pity party, I would switch into getting angry and blaming him for the cruelty and dishonesty he so willingly dished out. Mostly, though, even though his actions were narcissistic and cruel, I blamed myself for not being good enough. It was a repeat of Daddy. I wasn't lovable or he would have changed. But now, added to the unlovable me was the unsexy me, the unattractive me, and the bad mother me. It was overwhelming.

CHAPTER 14

ATTRACTING THE NARCISSIST

"My problem is I fall in love with words rather than actions. I fall in love with ideas and thoughts rather than reality."

- Jamie Clark

I had been working very hard for a construction company and the owner there knew I needed a lift. He said he would finance my home for me, just to make sure it was something I could afford. I was feeling very blessed and got a cute little two-bedroom condominium for me and my daughter. My divorce now final, I moved with my then 5 -year old to a different town for a new start, trying to put the pieces of myself back together.

I made friends with my new neighbor who was also divorced and had a son about my daughter's age. We decided to go out together one night to a club to dance. Once in the club, I was introduced to a handsome man who loved to dance and who was quite a charmer. I learned that he was very well to do financially and drove a Mercedes. That seemed good enough for me, so I decided to go all in. I gave him my number and it wasn't long before we were an item. I moved in with him and rented out my cute little condo. He seemed to have so much to offer. Little did I know that he was a narcissist and had been trained in the military in brainwashing techniques, which he would use on me to get what he wanted.

Of course, the exterior was just a façade; his life was in shambles. He claimed his ex-wife had tied up everything he had in court and his real estate brokerage was too much for him to handle. He spent his days lying on beaches flirting with women. I thought he was committed to making our relationship work, but I was soon to learn differently.

I went to real estate school to learn the ins and outs of his business. He wanted me to be his relocation agent, saying that's where we could make the most money. After I dug into the books it was clear that no one was minding the store, and I found embezzlement, among other things. The managing broker who had stepped in during his absence was prosecuted, and the two of us set out to rebuild the firm. I quit my job at the construction company and went to work every day to try to get the business back in shape.

He would come in and do very little and then leave for the beach, which began to make me resentful. His words told me how much he loved me and couldn't live without me, but his actions didn't seem to show it where it counted.

Then he made it clear that I was the woman for him and he wanted to have a baby together. I was delighted. A man who wanted my baby! He must really love me! We were excited and planning to get married if we were able to make it happen. I went off the pill.

Within two weeks he changed his tune. He said, "I'm not ready to be a father or get married." I explained that it didn't work that way, that I had been off the pill for two weeks and could already be pregnant. He told me to go back on the pill and I did, but several weeks later I knew I was already pregnant. When the doctor confirmed, I cried. I felt betrayed by him and by God. Why was I here? All I wanted was to love and be loved.

That evening I told him I was pregnant, hoping against hope that he would change his mind and be happy after all. He did the expected narcissistic move and ordered me to have an abortion. I said, "No."

CHAPTER 15

DEMONS, DEMONS EVERYWHERE!

Demons manifest themselves in people in different ways. For instance, out of nowhere, somebody can become very angry for no reason. That's not just an emotion. That's a demon.

- Stephen Baldwin

When I was 7 months pregnant, I was at the real estate office working on the books when my boyfriend ran in and screamed at me to throw him the keys. He seemed rattled. He ran and locked both plate glass doors. I asked him what was going on, and before he could answer a crazy man, foaming at the mouth and stark naked hit the side door. He was screaming obscenities. His eyes locked in on me and chills ran up and down my spine. He put his fist through ¾" safety glass. He grabbed the blinds and ripped them through trying to get in at me.

My boyfriend screamed to get out the back and opened the closet door which had an adjacency to the bathroom in the next suite. The closet was full of boxes and I tried desperately to climb over them, but scared and having a pregnant tummy in front of me made things difficult. I fell down. It was like a horror movie. And then, much to my amazement, my boyfriend climbed right over the top of me. I was aghast! Really? You climb over the woman carrying your baby? My heart sank. Was he going to leave me there to fend for myself?

Then he laughed a nervous laugh and reached back and told me to give him my hand. He pulled me through and then locked me in the bathroom and told me to stay there. I sat in that bathroom absolutely terrified of the unknown. He left me there. Was he getting help? Was he running away? I had no idea. All I could think of was that he climbed over me to get away. Who does that? I wanted to vomit but was trying to stay aware in case the crazy demonic man made it inside.

After a few minutes I heard the police sirens and loud speaker telling the crazy, naked man to get on the ground. I could hear them talking about putting him in the police car. I didn't know if I should wait or come out. Then my boyfriend came back to where I was hidden and told me the police wanted my statement.

There was absolutely no doubt that I was shook up. My body was shaking all over from the trauma. He led me by the hand to the police officer, and they walked me right past the police car where the man was in the back seat. He turned to me like a demon, staring at me and laughing hysterically. I thought I was going to pass out. It felt like I had met Charles Manson, but he had been convicted many years earlier. It was definitely the same energy, though. Absolutely, unequivocally, demonic power thrust on other people to kill them. This time, though, I was the target.

After giving the police my statement, I went home and went to bed. My body was in such trauma I couldn't take any more. I cried. I prayed. I asked God why this demon was after me. But I never got any answers until much later in life.

Within a few days we learned that the man had been jailed and had exhibited strange behavior, becoming Mussolini, Hitler and a few other "antichrist" types. He was then taken for a psychiatric evaluation. He passed and was released of his own recognizance awaiting trial. We learned he had been extradited from three other countries for this same type of behavior. He was to be extradited once again by the U.S. with absolutely no consequences for his actions, for the trauma inflicted on numerous people, and for the damage to the plate glass door and blinds in our building. I couldn't understand how any of this could even occur. It seemed literally insane. What I saw in that man's eyes was total insanity, and it was a look I would never forget.

Right now, the problem at hand was having this baby and deciding what to do. Should I stay with a coward who jumped over me to save himself?

CHAPTER 16

LIFE CHANGING DECISIONS

"It is hard to imagine a more stupid or more dangerous way of making decisions than by putting those decisions in the hands of people who pay no price for being wrong."

- Thomas Sowell

I stayed with the father of my child for another month and then moved back to my condominium with my older daughter. But once again the master manipulator pulled my heartstrings before the baby was born and got me to move back in. I wanted support. I wanted the baby to have a father. I was weak and afraid.

I had another little girl. She was beautiful. The delivery was a miracle. I felt nothing because she hit some nerve that stopped all pain during the final push. We named her and brought baby home. Within a couple weeks he was yelling at me saying he was going to have a vasectomy. I was shocked. Here was a man who thought he was punishing me by having a vasectomy because I gave birth to his child. All I could do was laugh as I cried inside. Did he really think I cared at this point?

Within the first two months after her birth, I left him and went out of state to my mother. I was exhausted. I was over emotional. I was in deep pain and hopelessness. My Mom did what she could and tried to talk me out of going back, but once again, in my weakness, I allowed him to talk me into coming back, saying he was wrong and he needed me to come back so he could prove his love to me and the baby.

I drove non-stop 16 hours with a 6-year old and a 3- month old in the car, arriving around nine o'clock at night. I was expecting a warm welcome. Instead, he wasn't home. He was at the local bar dancing and carousing with other women.

When I entered, I saw that his dog was in deep distress, and so I packed her up and got an emergency vet to help her. When I returned, he still wasn't home and came in after 2am. I was at wits end. All I could do was cry. How could I allow myself to be humiliated like this? This man didn't love me or the baby. He was only interested in himself and the moment. I felt like a fool.

I went deep into prayer, asking God to help me. All I could think was how stupid I was to fall for it again. What a bad mother I was to bring my children back into that kind of relationship. I was not worth anything. The only thing I had was two little babies that needed me, so I couldn't kill myself.

The next day I contacted a Christian Crisis Center and met a man who would be my role model and mentor for a number of years. He helped me understand the Bible and help me learn how to go directly to Scriptures to find my answers. I attended church twice a week and went to Sunday School faithfully. I began to grow in my faith. It was my direct connection to God and my friendships in the church that kept me going.

In the beginning, I found that particular church to be a hospital for the walking wounded. They knew that we had all fallen short in life and needed the love of God. I was a witness to miracle after miracle when that church was on fire for God.

Unfortunately, it didn't stay that way, the pastor falling prey to financial pledges and darkness from my baby's father. I felt betrayed by my church leaders, but I couldn't deny that I had experienced a deep love connection with my creator.

At that point, however, my perception of God was still outside of me. I saw Him as Big Daddy in the sky who was guiding me into right and wrong. I was still stuck in the good girl/bad girl paradigm.

Not long after that, I finally left the man for good. I moved back into my condominium and began again. The next few years were lived in the church with my two little girls. I became a fixture. I had friends. I had fun. And I met my next husband to be.

CHAPTER 17

MARRYING FOR ALL THE RIGHT REASONS

"I am good, but not an angel. I do sin, but I am not the devil. I am just a small girl in a big world trying to find someone to love."

- Marilyn Monroe

obby was a family kind of guy with two grown kids of his own. The difference in our ages seemed startling, but not by looking at us. He was 17 years my senior, but you couldn't tell when we were together. Bobby had always been a jock and never drank or smoked. He was a devout church attendee and ministry leader. He was handsome. He had it all! How lucky was I that we were together?

Our marriage lasted a year before he began punching walls. It was weird. The rage and anger had never shown up until after we were married. And somehow it was connected to sexuality and his mother.

After a knock down drag out fight, I went to the counselor I had been seeing. He told me that if I didn't leave this man who was abusing me that I was never to come back to his office. It was time for me to stop this emotional and now physical abuse pattern that seemed to plague me wherever I went.

I packed up my kids and headed back to Mom's. This time I stayed. We rented a home together and for another few years I lived and worked in another state minding my own business.

My husband and I talked occasionally, and once his kids graduated from high school, he was finally ready to make a move. We seemed to work out most of the issues, even though he hadn't really owned up to the abuse and decided we would try again. I couldn't bear the thought of another divorce.

We bought a home and were blessed with another baby girl. For seven years, I had the most wonderful marriage anyone could ask for. We couldn't go the day without calling each other to say we loved the other. We were so fulfilled. Then his mother died. Something snapped. He became abusive again. When he went after my teenage daughter to hit her with his fist, I jumped on him and knocked us both down the stairs. I got the kids in the car and left, called our pastor, and waited for help from the church.

The Pastor picked up Bobby and worked with him in his home to figure out what had made him snap. Eventually, he told me I was free to divorce after counseling indicated that he was incapable of facing the truth of his controlling and abusive behavior. But what was really scary was the night Bobby told me he wasn't who I thought he was. He had been living a completely double life.

It was my worst nightmare. How could this even happen? I was disillusioned. After 13 years of eating, sleeping and breathing God and church, my most intimate relationship had deteriorated leaving me feeling abused and separated from Creator. I had loved my husband unconditionally. I had created a beautiful home. How could this happen? Why was I meant to experience such darkness when I was serving God so completely? Why do bad things happen to good people?

I continued to spiral downward after my divorce, left the church and its judgments, and began singing at night with a professional keyboard player, the son of a Baptist Preacher, and a minister of music. It would be the worst decision of my life up until that point.

CHAPTER 18

DARK NIGHT OF THE SOUL

"I believe that the 'dark night of the soul' is a common spiritual experience. I believe, too, that the answer is continued seeking and perseverance. It helps to know that others have endured a loss of faith."

- Julia Cameron

Our relationship seemed to be on a new and higher path of truth. I was mesmerized by the spiritual side of his music. The beauty of his soul came to me in song in a way no one else ever had. Within three years, however, his alcoholism and abusive side became apparent, which triggered the same old fears in me, except now they had even become grander: I'm not good enough, I'm not loved, and I deserve to die. All these fears were operating on a subconscious level. It wasn't as if I heard myself saying those things. They were what I felt deeply within, without a conscious knowledge.

When I finally broke it off, I thought I could move on, but he stalked me and threatened my life. The system didn't support me with a restraining order, and within a few months, he broke into my home, beat and raped me and then attempted to kill me. I could hear angels whispering in my ear, directing me how to stay alive, and I did what they said.

For 4 hours, I was threatened, beaten, belittled, smothered until I was almost unconscious, raped and emotionally tortured, being told I was going to die. It was only after I convinced him to call my boss because he would suspect something was wrong, that I was able to scream "Help me! Call 911". Realizing the police were being called, he ran out the door after clobbering me one last time in the head with the phone. I managed to get up and lock the door, and then called 911.

The policeman showed up and found me confused and terrified; not making too much sense. After talking for a few minutes, he looked me straight in the eyes and said, "I don't believe you."

That catapulted me into even more terror! It triggered my other biggest fear: I am not being seen and heard. I almost died and he doesn't believe me! I told the officer I wasn't going to talk to him anymore and to leave my home, as I sobbed. He called a rape specialist, and she appeared on the scene with compassion. I was in such a state of shock over the system having failed me on so many levels, that I refused to take it any further. My psyche couldn't take any more in the moment. I refused a rape test and I wouldn't go to the hospital. I just wanted it all to be over. I wanted to be left alone to lick my wounds.

The report was made. I called a friend and spent the night at his house. I chose a man because I knew I needed to be safe, and another woman couldn't help much against the aggressions of an insane man. My dear friend told me I was beautiful and that I didn't deserve it, and held me all night as I cried. I will be eternally grateful for his tenderness and compassion in my darkest hour.

After I came out of shock and got treatment for the physical trauma my body had suffered, I went to the District Attorney and told my story. It took about 3 months for them to find my perpetrator, this man I had once deeply loved. He finally talked with the police and ended up confessing to the same officer who didn't believe me. A trial found him guilty and sentenced him to 4 years in prison for breaking and entering with the intent to commit a violent act. It seems that to convict someone of rape in that state jurors needed 100% agreement for a rape conviction. Because I didn't go to the hospital, and because we had a prior relationship, my case was suspect.

Just before the sentencing, after being nudged by my intuition, I opened the crawlspace door on the floor of the closet in my bedroom. There was DNA evidence where my perpetrator had been hiding under my house. I called the police and they took the DNA evidence and gave all the information to the judge.

I know that nudge was Creator's protection. Without that evidence, he might have gotten off completely. It was my word against his, even with a confession (because he later refuted it, saying it was offered under duress). I shudder when I think that I was being spied upon as I slept. It's a very sad story, yes. And yet now I understand how my subconscious mind had drawn in the perfect person to fit with my belief system that I wasn't enough and deserved to die. As the subconscious victim, I found the perfect perpetrator to reflect my victim consciousness. Still, at that point in time, I didn't understand it was me who was bringing it all about on a subconscious level. I still needed to learn my worth and value before I could accept that I was **playing the role** of the victim. It would be a few years before I learned just how strong I really was, how to create boundaries, and how to avoid recreating abuse and trauma in my life.

After the trial, I needed to start over in another state. I was offered admittance into the witness protection program, yet because I was working on a public singing career, it didn't make much sense. After moving to Southern California with $200 in my pocket, I sought a new job, with new hope and focus. I was determined to become financially successful and create a home for my young teenage daughter. I was determined to create something different than what my older two daughters had experienced; one who was now a police dispatcher and another in college becoming a certified holistic practitioner.

I finally began to take control of my life, instead of being a victim of it. I forged a new path that felt great, finding a job at a radio station that paid me more in commissions than I could have ever earned in a salaried job. Even better, it utilized my artistic gifts, my marketing abilities and my ability to feel intuitively what clients needed. I was finally on the right path! I was making money, really focused on creating a solid financial foundation for me and my youngest daughter. Finally, I was able to go beyond some of the pain and trauma I had left in another state. This time, I was determined to succeed!

CHAPTER 19

THE MIND-BODY-SPIRIT CONNECTION
FACING DEATH AFTER FACING DEATH!

"Three things cannot be long hidden: the sun, the moon, and the truth."

- The Buddha

M y new path was paying off. I worked hard and focused on creating financial success, making more money than I ever had before. Emotionally, I was choosing to put my past behind me, which meant not focusing on it. Unfortunately, my body was still stuck in old trauma. Within a year I was hospitalized and told I had six months to live.

My body was toxic. Doctors told me that my entire large intestine needed to be completely removed. Interesting that the emotional components attributed to the large intestine are low self-esteem and shame. Well there it is! I don't know any woman who has gone through the terror of rape and near death who doesn't have feelings of worthlessness and shame. It would be something I needed to work on to get those stuck emotions out of my body. Since it seemed to be a lifelong theme, I would embark on a journey that would last for years as I learned how to let go of these lies about the truth of who I AM.

Over the course of that year, I came face to face with death and made choices for myself that would put me back on the path toward my destiny. *Funny how facing death has a way of waking you up to the truth of your life!*

Talk about a metaphor. The colon is that which eliminates waste and toxins. When it becomes toxic, it freezes or shuts down. It is also within the solar plexus, the energy center in the body that processes and feels tension, fear and emotion. It hit me in the gut, literally! I had allowed toxic people into my life, and they reflected back my hatred of myself perfectly. The continued allowance of abuse went directly into my colon. I held on to the disgust, the shame, the fear that I was nothing, proving to myself that I didn't count, wasn't worth anything, and deserved to die. My physical body was simply revealing my internal toxic life with myself. To make matters worse, I hadn't eaten healthy foods, and lived on diet sodas, hamburgers, pizza and never drank water. I was dehydrated on a cellular, emotional and spiritual level! I made choices to harm myself; my colon simply complied.

Luckily, this time I trusted my intuition and contacted a natural healer, rather than listening to the medical doctors. Having my entire large intestine removed was the kiss of death, and I knew it. My natural doctor. gave me the same prognosis of six months to live but said if I was willing to do everything he said, and was willing to change my lifestyle, he could save my colon and restore my health. I gave him a resounding "YES" and began a journey to heal myself holistically; mind, body and spirit. He guided me through each critical process of healing as it occurred. It was a dance, and I was learning to listen to my body and what it was telling me. Each phase of my healing was critical. I'm grateful that he was in my life and was a champion for my health.

My boyfriend at the time was so kind and nurturing that when my health was restored, oddly I felt that I owed him, and I agreed to marry, knowing that he was capable of abuse. But he was another musician who wrote and performed with me, toured with me, and again, was a huge contrast of the lightest of light and the darkest of dark. For whatever reason, I continued my pattern and married someone who continued to reflect my lack of love for myself. Crazy, right? But it was familiar. We do things over and over until we can completely let go of the victim within. Most deeply rooted emotional change happens in steps. This step, for me, was better than the last. Three steps forward, two steps back.

At one point, my doctor had turned me over to an associate. As curriculum designer and professor at a massage school, he understood body mechanics and mind-body connection better than anyone I had ever met. He talked to me about psychic pain. I knew intuitively that I had lots of it, but I didn't have a clue had to get it out of my body.

With cranial sacral therapy I went into primal scream, releasing energy so strongly that my body literally shook. It was intense, like I had released torture of some kind. It was confounding, and it took me a couple of days to integrate what had happened. My health took a huge leap forward again, and I began to have visions of myself being tortured in other times. Since it wasn't from this lifetime, I wasn't sure what it was, but I could see it plainly in my mind's eye, like a movie. The visions always came through when I was deeply relaxed. Because my doctor had forewarned me that I might see things that don't make sense, none of it scared me. I intuitively knew it was all part of the release and I didn't attach to the pain. I was able to observe myself like I was outside my body, completely devoid of emotion. It was the first time I felt this kind of detachment, and it seemed healthy to me. One of the greatest things that this doctor did for me was to tell me that it was time that I knew I was a Mercedes, not a broken-down Volkswagen, and to pull the title out of my glove box and take a look. What a metaphor!

He believed in and saw the authentic Alison Astara, and it changed my life. I will be forever grateful and want to pass on that belief to you. The truth is we are ALL luxury cars driving around thinking we are "beaters". I want to be your cheerleader for the truth of your luxury!

The next few years, my life began to undergo a complete change. I had become extremely successful in my career, and in hindsight, had gone completely into my masculine energy in order to survive in a "man's world". The corporate environment is definitely cutthroat, and while I worked for a private broadcasting network, it was no different than any other corporation after it went public. The people became not much more than a means to meeting the projections given to Wall Street, rather than human beings with families. I was working hard at being successful, and I had found my niche, so I was doing well financially, but longed to be a woman.

At home, I wanted to relax into the arms of my man, but to my dismay, I had taken on the masculine role, and he the more passive, feminine role. I wonder now if I had gone so completely into my masculine that he had to balance our relationship. Who knows. I think what ultimately happened was he lost his self-esteem because he wasn't fulfilling himself in his own work. As a result, he began to feel no self -accomplishment, and started belittling me, and picking fights. It wasn't long before the relationship was completely out of control.

CHAPTER 20

CHECKING OUT ONCE
AND FOR ALL

"Any psychologist will tell you that healing comes from honest confrontation with our injury or with our past. Whatever that thing is that has hurt us or traumatized us, until we face it head on, we will have issues moving forward in a healthy way"

- Nate Parker

In addition to dealing with the health crisis with my intestines, my life was so out of balance between work and home that I fell on the steps in my backyard and hit the back of my head on the concrete. Of course, I didn't know I was out of balance. I just considered myself under heavy stress.

The impact of my head hitting the concrete was so severe that I received a double concussion; the first on the back of the brain from the impact; the second on the front of the brain where my brain was bruised when it catapulted forward, slamming into my own skull, causing concussion #2. My C-1 or Atlas, the seat of the skull, was knocked 45 degrees to the right. In essence, my head was off my body.

I was very lucky not to have severed a carotid artery. In the hospital, I remember almost passing out as I turned my head, realizing I was in deep trouble. I lost most of the hearing in my right ear, as the bones in the inner ear were completely fractured. I had also damaged the nerves to the ear when the brain pulled them forward as it was catapulted into my skull. I was told the only way to restore my hearing on that side was with hearing aids, at least until they had figured out a way regrow the little hairs on the nerve endings that I had damaged.

There were several interesting things that happened as a result of that injury that would change my life forever. First, I remember dying and coming back. While I was unconscious only a short time, I remember being asked to continue my lifetime and to remember my worth and value. I said I would, and I awoke. My daughter, who had seen me fall, had called the paramedics, and they were there quickly. I found it interesting that they were adamant with their questioning me about abuse. They were convinced my husband had pushed me. While he had not (he was upstairs in our bedroom) they had picked up the energy of abuse all around me. I assured them he had not pushed me but that I had fallen on the step off the porch. It just goes to prove that the vibration of abuse can't be hidden. People pick it up, no matter how we try to hide it.

I would never be the same again after that injury. I had literally died and come back. I had been in the presence of Creator Source. I was given a promise that my life would change, but it took quite some time before I would be able to understand exactly what that meant.

I spent the next six months working on getting out of the black hole. I had what they call "boxer's head" which means your entire world is right up in your face. I was so claustrophobic I couldn't breathe! It was so bad that I refused an MRI. I knew that even with an open MRI and drugs, I wouldn't be able to make it without having a complete panic attack. The neurologist told me that it was clear that the impact had hit the emotional part of my brain. One minute I felt like a little girl who wanted to hide in a corner and cry, and the next minute I wanted to kill. There were no reasons for any of my behavior. It was a result of brain swelling. As a result of that experience, I now know and have compassion for people who are bi-polar, understanding the depth of despair it brings. Words can't even describe it!

I was fortunate enough to have been referred by my champion of doctors to someone with an Accuscope. It is known for clearing physical trauma to the central nervous system. After one session I felt like I came back. This practitioner referred me to an atlas chiropractor to get the C-1 (atlas) back into place, and I was on the road to recovery. I had lost my photographic memory, and my short-term memory, but I had been given gifts that were still yet to be revealed. I persevered.

Recovering from brain trauma was not easy. There were so many frustrations over not being able to remember the simplest of things... like a phone number. I couldn't dial a complete phone number without looking at the numbers one by one. I couldn't repeat a number at all, and for someone who had up until that time had a photographic memory, you can bet I was frustrated. To make matters worse, things on the home front had deteriorated. The more I played the victim, the more he played the perpetrator. It was a vicious circle.

As a result of my brain trauma, my entire endocrine system went on pause. My glands were in shock, not knowing how to overcome the trauma. One day about 6 months later, my husband had to carry me into the x-ray department to see why I couldn't walk. I thought it was kidney stones, but was very surprised to find out that I had grown a tumor the size of a small baby inside my womb, and it was so large it was pressing against all the nerves in back and shutting off the flow of my kidneys. An emergency hysterectomy was ordered. I was so depressed that I really began questioning Creator as to why I chose to come back. I was in massive pain, and my youngest daughter who had lived with us had left to live with her Dad, explaining that she couldn't stand to see me allow myself to be victimized any longer. What a wake-up call!

I believe that was the final straw. When my youngest daughter told me the truth, I knew I wasn't hiding anything. My daughters, once again, were the only love I had in my life, and yet I had so let them down by not knowing how to love myself. I was ashamed and angry with myself all at the same time.

After the hysterectomy, I was told that they also removed one ovary with abnormal growths, but there was no indication of cancer. I was relieved.

One day I was visiting my MD who was working on my hormones after the hysterectomy. He said he noticed I was emotionally down and asked if he could help. I told him I just wasn't happy, and that life, even though I was successful, wasn't what I thought it should be. He sent me to a person he knew who was a spiritual guide. He said just to trust him, and I would thank him later.

My first visit to this spiritual guide was miraculous. She was able to see the abuse around me and seemed compassionate and understanding as I sobbed uncontrollably. Just then, a white light came down just like a spotlight, and seemed to shine around me and through me. It was pure love, and I was held directly in the arms of Creator. She told me that Creator was with me and was helping me to grow spiritually. She became my teacher for many years, and I will be eternally grateful for the wisdom and love she bestowed. She was the first person I had ever met that could feel the angels and see the angels and Jesus like I could when I was a kid. There was definitely a lot to learn, and it started me on a path of discovering how I could get more of the love I had experienced in those first few meetings with her. After working with her for a few months, I began to realize that divorce must happen if I was to survive. It was the first time in my life that I cared enough about myself to make a choice for me and not everyone else. I learned many important lessons by going through the divorce, particularly about money. It was time I let Creator take control of EVERYTHING.

During that three-year period of discovering my mind-body-spirit connection, I also found a meditation workshop that was based in angelic assistance to seek the truth of my existence. It went beyond the many years of religious training. To this day, I still deeply value my religious training and know it has shaped and molded my experience with Creator. I understand now that I was ready to go to the next level of consciousness, and what I heard during that meditation was startling.

I'll never forget that day, sitting in a class with a meditation guide who claimed to be able to connect to angels. It felt right to reconnect to that ability and to see if I could find some more answers about myself. In spite of my financial accomplishments, I still felt alone and unloved. I had just overcome an illness that should have killed me. I should have been happy, but I wasn't. I worried I would never find love.

Our facilitator guided us on through an exercise of grounding with the Earth and connecting to our Creator in the spiritual realm. She encouraged us to feel the connection of that relationship. Angels were our guides into the Temple of Records, which I understood to be the writings and truth of everything that has ever existed and will ever exist in the future. I saw what was like a movie starring me, going down the hallway of this Temple to a specific book. That large book had my name on it. Then our human guide told us to ask the question, "Who am I?" As I kept my eyes closed and continued to watch this movie in my mind's eye, my heavenly guide opened the book of Elyce and pointed to large words on the printed page, which said "I AM LOVE".

I began to sob. For someone who had been seeking unconditional love all her life and not found it, it was the most profound answer I could have ever been given. I began to understand that I am completely connected to divine love, I AM love and that nothing can ever change that, no matter how I feel, no matter what circumstances I am in. Love was INSIDE of me, not something outside of me that I needed to find. After years of over-giving to get, I learned that the most important thing in life was to love and accept myself. The love I so desperately wanted was within me and WAS me. I saw myself radiantly beautiful, with white robes, gold trim, and large angel's wings. It was the authentic divine self I had forgotten for many years.

This revelation gave me power and hope. I saw the illusion in what I had formerly believed about myself. I no longer felt separate from Creator; instead, I felt one with Creator. It gave me a sense of purpose and propelled me on a journey to experience myself in a new and authentic way. If I lived my life authentically, I would experience love because I AM love. What a concept! All I needed was to BE the truth of who I AM. I needed to BELIEVE the truth about my authentic self.

After many years of personal discovery, my search for authenticity has grown even more deeply. I've learned how to gracefully let go of things that aren't in alignment with loving myself, and that by loving myself, I am also loving Creator. I ended my abusive marriage and began working on myself. I began to make amends to my daughters for my playing the victim and having taught them to do the same. I sought to mend every relationship that had ever been strained, so I could be clean and clear before Creator. I have spent the last 20 years clearing the old and receiving the new.

The "gifts" that Creator had promised began to make themselves known as I proceeded in my studies. I found I was clairaudient, which means I can hear the spiritual realm. I can actually hear Creator, Jesus and the Angels and Ascended Masters speaking with me directly. I became clairvoyant and claircognizant. That simply means I can see with my mind's eye the spiritual realm, and have instant knowledge from Creator, not knowing how I got it. The biggest gift, which I had always had, was that of clairsentience. I had empathic abilities to feel energies of other people and experience them. I had been doing this since I was a little girl, without understanding my overly-empathic abilities and how I had taken on so much of other peoples' illness and suffering. Once I understood them, these gifts all helped me to connect to the spiritual realms of light so deeply that I can transmit the energies of Divine Love and Light for others. This is what I spend my time doing now, and it is amazing work. I see people change right before my eyes, feeling loved, making good choices, and serving humanity in astounding ways. While my head injury seemed to set me back, the angels tell me that because of the head injury I don't doubt what I hear and see. My mind has been re-calibrated not to doubt the truth of Spirit. As a result, I simply follow what I am guided to do, and my life has become an adventure. I'm now the female version of Indiana Jones! I travel to the world's sacred places, listen to what the Spirit Guides tell me took place, and work with them to heal the Earth and any traumas that occurred against the people.

I have become the perpetual learner, with no answers. Now I live in the question, and open up to face my blind spots, old wounds and traumas that controlled my life for so long. Living this kind of life journey isn't always easy. It takes a deep sense of honesty with yourself and others, but in the end, it is always worth it. By continuing on the path of self-love, I am supported by Creator, the Angels and Masters to bring me through the control patterns my ego self creates. And synchronicity began to happen as I let go of doing things my own way. Everything started coming together. I became more trusting of Spirit and the Universe, knowing that I would be given answers that I couldn't work out in my logical mind. I learned that you can't think outside the box when you are inside the box!

Through all the trauma and illness, I've learned that there are always new things to learn, and lessons in understanding and exhibiting compassion for myself and others. There are also completely new ways of perceiving the spiritual realm and the human realm. The journey of rediscovering the authentic self is an exciting adventure. You never know what's next, and it's always better than what you dreamed! That is Creator's gift that lies beyond the darkness in our lives.

I've learned principles about how the cosmos really works that have enabled me to accept and love myself, forgive myself for my mistakes, and to BE authentic in all situations. It's an eternal process, and it's not something we finish until we are able to complete all our lessons and merge back with our Creator. If you consider and apply these principles yourself, they will literally change everything in your life for the better. They will unlock the truth within you, and you will begin to create an entirely new reality for yourself. You'll find peace, love and happiness from within, and so it will be manifest without. If I can do it, you can too!

CHAPTER 21

GIFTS FROM EGYPT

"(Egypt) is a great place for contrasts: splendid things gleam in the dust."

- Gustave Flaubert

After several years of healing myself and working with Spiritual Masters in this realm and beyond the veil, my primary Angelic Guide came in quite profoundly as I was returning from a trip to Boston. I had a vision on the plane. I went into deep meditation and found myself inside Giza Pyramid. I was with 2 friends. We were very low in the base of the pyramid, but I was guiding the three of us and was told to go deeper into the underground of the pyramid.

As I climbed deeper and deeper into the pyramid we were locked into a chamber. We were all afraid that we would never find our way out of the pyramid. Then I was told to look into a specific spot between the rocks. I did, and there I uncovered some secret scrolls. I opened the scrolls and the pyramid opened into a magic chamber of light. Then my body jerked and I was brought back to my 3D reality.

What was this vision? What did it mean?

It wasn't long before I decided I must go to Egypt to find out what was awaiting me there. The vision seemed to be some kind of key.

I had no idea how I could go to a foreign country or who I would go with. I prayed for God to bring me a companion and guide and to show me the way. And I waited.

Within a month I met and began dating a man who had actually lived in Egypt and knew his way around. We seemed to really go deep fast (one of my fatal flaws) so I asked him if he was interested in going to Egypt with me. He said he would be honored. It wasn't long before we moved in together and I began to feel safe and secure.

Then one day I received an invitation from a woman who was leading tours in Egypt to come on her tour. I didn't know this woman, so I was surprised how she got my name. I contacted her and she said she didn't know.... I wasn't on her mailing list! But she said, "Obviously, you are supposed to come or this email wouldn't have been redirected to you!"

I checked in with my angelic guides and they laughingly told me that yes, they had redirected the invitation and they wanted me to go. So it was full speed ahead! I purchased this woman's books and began to read about her. I also began doing deep meditations with my guides who were telling me exactly what would happen when I got to Egypt. The instructions were profound. I would be accompanied by Jesus, Mother Mary, Mary Magdalene and several archangels. I would make connections to the Egyptian Gods and Goddesses so that I would understand the energy of what was needed, and the tour guide and I would be doing a deep work that would change the world. The only condition was that I wasn't to tell anyone any of the specifics. Not even the tour guide! I was just supposed to allow it to roll out by its own design, knowing and trusting that Spirit was guiding every minute. I had a friend who was a hypnotherapist and coach record my conversations with the guides from the other side so that I would remember my mission.

The whole thing seemed like something beyond anything I could have imagined. Was I nuts? Was I going to Egypt in some kind of deluded state? Regardless, I had to find out. I told my boyfriend/ companion that I had been given some very detailed instructions about the nature of my mission and that I wasn't even supposed to tell the tour guide, but that she and I would be doing deep work together that would be brought about by Spirit.

He wasn't a spiritual guy, but he believed me and supported me. That was all I needed.

The day came when we finally arrived at the Egyptian airport awaiting our driver to pick us up at the hotel. We knew our airline was flying us in a couple hours after they started the "Welcome" from our host. When we arrived at the hotel, the meeting was just breaking up. We watched as more than 30 people filed out of the room. I was in shock! More than 30 people on this tour and I was supposed to meet and do world-changing work with someone I didn't know? Hmmm. I wondered how that would ever come to pass but checked my disbelief at the door and tucked in for the night, having no opportunity to even meet our guide.

The next morning, we had breakfast and were loaded into a tour bus, where we spent the day at the Egyptian Museum (which was fascinating) and different tourist shops. We were told by our bus leader that we were to meet our tour host that evening at 7pm sharp in the hotel lobby and that we were going to the Sphinx for the multimedia show.

My companion and I were in the lobby promptly at 7pm only to discover that they had already all left, and we were given the wrong information by our bus leader. We got in a cab and tried to find the group, but it was no use. The cab driver kept taking us to KFC! My companion and I got in a bit of an argument and headed back to the hotel. We were both frustrated and worn out and angry that we had not been given the right information.

As I waited at the bar, I held back the tears and asked my guides what was going on. I doubted myself and my revelations and called myself an idiot. And yet, I still felt internally that everything was oddly right on track. It confused me, to say the least.

When the group returned, my companion went straight to the tour host and gave her a piece of his mind. He was quite upset and told her that I had some wild idea that I was on some sort of spiritual mission and now I was upset and crying, and he was livid at her for not providing appropriate instructions for the people on tour. She apologized to him and came straight to the bar and sat down next to me.

Her words were somewhat of a shock. She simply said, "You weren't supposed to be there."

I turned and asked her why. She said it was a hokey tourist trap that the management company had put together and she was sort of embarrassed that she had allowed it, not knowing what it was. She said it would have lowered my opinion of the tour had I gone because it wasn't a spiritual message at all, but rather a very secular event. We began to get to know each other over a few drinks and became fast friends. I simply told her I was there to do deep spiritual work and was told by Spirit not to reveal its nature. She said she understood and that we would let it unfold.

The first part of our itinerary was to fly to Luxor and take a boat down the Nile, visiting all the Temples as we traveled. My experience of Luxor Temple was absolutely amazing, as I walked between the colossal columns and felt each chakra turn on from my root to my crown. As I finally entered the crown chakra (which was the ancient holy of holies where only the King and his Priest or Priestess could go) I closed my eyes and went into deep meditation. I remember feeling completely safe, surrounded by Egyptian gods and goddesses. It was so different! Jesus, Mother Mary and Mary Magdalene were with me as well, and I soon understood that Mother Mary's energy was the same as their goddess Isis, and Mary Magdalene's energy was very similar to that of the goddess Hathor. Jesus' energy felt like the god Horus! The similarities were unmistakable. I could feel each energy in my body and understood that this was simply the Egyptian expression of my Christian gods and goddesses.

When I came out of my deeply meditative state I found a police officer standing guard over me. It was as if Spirit had provided the protection I needed while going on my journey. I had lost track of my companion, and there was both immense light and immense dark in this place. The darkness revealed itself through the men in turbans along the corridors as they called out to women to come join them. It felt very unsafe and sexual in nature. Later I learned that one of the naïve girls on our trip had gone up to one of these men only to have herself thrust up against the wall in the shadows and manhandled. Whether or not she was raped I wasn't sure, but she certainly got a taste of the dark side of the Temples. We were all warned again not to follow anyone and to stay with companions at all times.

The other really astounding revelation at Luxor Temple was seeing the orbs and energy appear in the photos were taking. We would take photos of carvings in the temples and when we looked at the image there were hundreds of floating orbs and streams of energy in the photos! It was quite remarkable!

The next remarkable day was our trip to Abydos Temple. This temple had special significance to our host, as she had once spent the night in the section called "Isis Temple" and had had visions appear. This was also where the famous Osiron was underneath the Temple, which was supposedly the tomb of Osiris. There had been a natural stream that had flowed from the temple of Osiris for hundreds of years. When we arrived, the government had taken over the gardens and paved much of the area toward the temple. The stream had stopped flowing. Our host was beside herself in tears, crying that they had destroyed the flow of energy to the temple. I suggested that we try to restore it. The next thing I knew she ordered the other 30 members of our group to go underneath the Temple to the Osiron and pray and invited me to the Isis Temple above to see what work Spirit would have us to do.

As we clasped arms and began our deep meditation, the room began to change. All of a sudden, I felt a surge of powerful light come beaming though my body. My host looked at me in awe. I was hearing my guides telling me to "Hold the Light". I told her what they were telling me every step of the way, and she knew her piece. She called up the priests who had been trapped beneath the Temple for thousands of years and called upon Isis to assist us to free them. I could see nothing but light and felt like I was a transformer as she talked with the priests and priestesses who were refusing to go into the light because they felt it was their duty to protect the temple. The light source within me coaxed and guided them into crossing, and I witnessed many souls and a baby being handed from the underground into the light. All I knew was that I was a beacon of light and that it was so powerful that I knew I was in what was described as my rainbow body, or light body.

My host and I did a ceremony to bring back the water, and next thing I knew I was back in my body and the people on the tour were sitting all around me. That moment I only noticed one woman who would be on my other side each time the transmission came through me.

We didn't talk about the event and what happened between us until later the next day while floating down the Nile on our boat. The experience was so sacred we needed to allow it to percolate within us. We met privately and confirmed our experiences. My host confirmed that she could see right through me when I became the light. She said it was like a bright light that made me completely translucent. My hair was flying in a breeze, and bright light beamed out of me, filling the room. I told her that Horus and Hathor and Isis (the energies of Jesus, Mary Magdalene and Mary) were speaking with me as I became the light and the feelings I had were that of complete divine love. She asked if I saw the souls who had been released. I explained that I had seen souls flying to heaven but that was all. I didn't know who they were. My job was to "be the light" and her job was to release those souls. We reveled in the experience, and held it close to our hearts. We were eager to see what the rest of the trip would reveal. I told her that the Gods told me that the water would be coming back to the Osirion soon. She said we would see. It is my understanding that the water did come back not long after our ceremony.

The next miracle occurred when we were at the Temple of Karnak. We were visiting the long-closed Temple of Sekhmet and weren't sure we were going to be able to get in. Our Egyptian guides paid the security officers bakshish (bribes) and we were permitted to enter.

As I entered the area I had a strange connection to everything that existed. There were wild dogs were running around the grounds and I could hear them communicating like I knew what they were saying. Yeshua (Jesus) was my guide into the temple, and I felt completely in the power of the Holy Spirit. I prayed on the entire trip to the temple, and knew that something big was about to happen.

We would take turns in groups of 5 or 6 to enter the temple. It was a small temple, where Sekhmet, the female warrior with the head of a lion was said to have descended into the underworld to heal souls and proclaim war with the darkness.

When my group entered, our host told me privately that she would unlock the portal to the underworld so that I could do my work. I had no idea what that meant, until I gazed upon the statue of Sekhmet and she came alive.

As I focused on her, her eyes opened and she looked at me and nodded her head. It was as if she was looking right through me. She was happy that I was there, and said that I was welcome. I felt like I was living a dream. Then our host said some prayers and did some chanting, and I saw the underground open and a large ancient boat appeared. I rode the boat into the underworld, and soon I found myself walking through what I thought were the Halls of Amenti. It was lit in emerald green with doors down a long corridor. I knew exactly where to go and turned right to enter the darkest of rooms where I could only see two red eyes peering at me in the darkness. It was freezing cold, and I could feel the darkness all around me. I found myself saying things to the beast that I was being prompted to say. I thanked him for his service and told him his time had come to an end. It was now time to release the people from his hold and allow the ushering in of the feminine back to the planet. It seemed like I spoke quite a discourse, and there was agreement.

Then the next thing I can recall I was standing in the original place where we started. I opened my eyes and only the host and myself were there. I held up my arms and there was an earthquake. My entire body was shaking from the inside out. It was as if all the energy that was being released from the darkness was also being released from my body. And at that moment, I saw thousands of souls, looking like whisps of energy, flying upward toward the heavens.

Just then I felt the hosts arms around me and we hugged and sobbed. She said, "That's why we came. It is done."

I could barely stand up. I asked her where everyone went, and she said she sent them out when she saw I went underground. It was once again just her and me, as my guides had indicated before I ever came to Egypt. She held space for me until I could return, and I wonder now if what we did that day caused the Arab Spring movement. I believe it just may have. And women began to stand up and be counted in Egypt like never before.

With all that we had accomplished, the task was not yet complete. The biggest event of my life was just about to take place… in the Giza Pyramid.

CHAPTER 22

TRAVELING BEYOND TIME

"In Einstein's equation, time is a river. It speeds up, meanders, and slows down. The new wrinkle is that it can have whirlpools and fork into two rivers. So, if the river of time can be bent into a pretzel, create whirlpools and fork into two rivers, then time travel cannot be ruled out."

- Michio Kaku

We boarded our tour buses at 4:00am to be at the pyramids at very early dawn. We were to go in two groups of 15. My group was the first group in. We were not allowed cameras or phones or anything but ourselves inside the pyramid. Guards were everywhere.

The host went in first, saying she was going to open the portal so the pyramid would come alive. Then we all began to make the climb up the narrow wooden make-shift stairs at a ridiculous angle that sometimes forced you to bend down and climb through tight spaces. We had to stop several times as people needed to rest and breathe from the climb. It was definitely intense! And then at the very top, you had to climb through on your hands and knees into the Kings Chamber.

Once we were inside the Kings Chamber it was a sight to behold. There was an open space serving as a window, and our guide pointed out the belt of Orion and the angle of the star Sirius in alignment with the pyramid. It was significant, I would learn in days to come.

Then we created a large circle around the room and around the King's sarcophagus, which was open and inviting.

The host said we were to begin with an invocation of thanksgiving and then we would do sounding to complete the opening of the portals beyond time.

The 15 people in that room sounded like a choir of angels. I was astounded at the voluminous, beautiful sounds that were coming from inside that chamber. It wasn't long before I realized that we had been joined by choirs of angels, and that the sounds that we could hear were differentiating the frequencies of each person who was taking their turn lying in the sarcophagus.

In ancient Egypt, it is believed that the Pharaohs may have used these sarcophagi to time travel throughout the cosmos. I certainly was interested in that and was eager to see if I could do it myself. But while I awaited my turn, I listened intently to the sounds of the choir and the harmonic tones and the dissonant tones that revealed themselves with different people. It was as if the energy of who they were was creating the vibrational frequency of the sound. It was truly amazing and informative. Those on the journey who seemed to be angry, pushy, or had a "me first" attitude seemed to bring through dissonant tones and vibrations. You could hear where they were just "off".

I watched as each one of them climbed into the sarcophagus. Our host did prayers and energy work over the top of them and spoke with them as they were in the sarcophagus. Within about 5 minutes, they were complete, and they would climb back out to join the group. Some of them seemed to be lighter, almost with halos around them when they returned. It was quite a sight to see!

When it was my turn, I prayed diligently to be cleared of all fear and asked that I would be able to transmute it and transform into my light body and travel through time. It wasn't long before I felt like I felt in Abydos… the light completely taking over my body, feeling like a beacon of light inside the sarcophagus. Then I had a vision of Thoth standing next to a stargate that was the shape of the vesica pisces. I knew this symbol! It was the doorway my artist friend had painted for me indicating it was a gift that would be my "doorway" to the angelic realm! Thoth asked me if I was ready, and I said "Yes" without hesitation. I immediately felt like I was on a space ship and that's the last I remember. It would be several minutes before I returned to my body. I felt completely different, filled with light and shaking again like I had each time with this experience of being filled with light. I climbed out of the sarcophagus, and the host said, "You did it again. This time you completely turned into light and then disappeared."

The experience was so extraordinary that it can't be described. Photos of me taken over the next few days seemed to show me glowing with golden light. I felt absolutely wonderful, beautiful, and completely at peace. I still felt attached to the starship, and for days, felt it following me. I still don't understand it, but I know that somehow on that day I was able to have an experience beyond this realm into the next, and it was more divine than any experience I have ever had. I will spend the rest of my life pondering the feelings of that magical moment.

When we all exited the pyramid, I walked around all three pyramids and simply felt the grounds. I picked up a stone and put it in my pocket as a reminder of my time travels. It stays on my altar to this day to remind me that there is much more than we will ever know about creation and our creator, but sometimes we can touch it and feel it and know that it changes us for the better.

I can say now that that moment gave me a glimpse of "The Me I Couldn't See" who was a beautiful, divine being of light. Once you have that experience, a calm encircles you and you know who you truly are. It is the true meaning of Authenticity. Both "The Me I Couldn't See" who was fearful, abused, and acting as a victim and "The Me I Couldn't See" who was divine taught me the truth of who I AM. A divine spirit in a human body. And both are beautiful.

And with that being said, now it's time for me to give you some keys to unlock both of them inside you! The following chapters go deeply into methods of finding your authenticity. They are not fictional. They are tried and true, and taken from personal experience. Take the time to use the next few chapters as possibilities for you to go to the next level of yourself. You can do it!

CHAPTER 23

WHAT BLOCKS AUTHENTICITY?

"Your Largest Fear Carries Your Greatest Growth"

- Unknown

The biggest block to authenticity is fear. According to Neale Donald Walsh, the acronym for fear is "false evidence appearing real." That false evidence is what triggers the feeling you get when you are in a panic or overwhelmed with your circumstances. It feels very real and threatening, even though it is simply an illusion that has been filtered through an old wound or trauma. Fear wears many faces. It can show up as panic, anger, hopelessness, overwhelm, aggression, superiority, inferiority, passivity, negativity, and more. So what creates this fear?

The ultimate human fear is based in the belief system that we are alone and separate from our Creator. It is connected to the fear of death, because of the genetic pattern of having forgotten the truth that we are eternal co-creators. We don't die, we simply change form when our bodies die and merge back to original Source energy. This fear of death and separateness was what I kept trying to overcome. My spirit kept calling forth the people and circumstances for me to discover that I wasn't separate, that Creator and the Angels were with me and protected me. I have learned that I have had to create extreme circumstances for me to see the lesson! Through these lessons of fear of death, I became empowered to help others heal from fears that create disease, broken relationships, career problems, money issues and more. Healing fear within is the biggest catalyst toward becoming authentic.

It was very interesting when a number of years after all the major trauma, I found a book called "Gene Keys" by Richard Rudd. It was a hologenetic transmission that assists people into catalyzing their DNA. What was exciting was that it gave me insight into my life's purpose and my life's work. My life's purpose was the 38th Gene Key. In the shadow state, it is one of the darkest gene keys there is, and creates struggle between light and dark until it is accepted. Once the Shadow of Struggle is embraced and accepted within oneself, you receive the gift of perseverance. I certainly had gone through that journey! And after the gift comes the Siddhi of Honor, which holds all beings in a state of Honor. It's giving yourself up for another, no matter how dark. It's unconditional love. What a revelation for me. It was totally my journey! I even went into the underground in the Temple of Sekhmet to face the darkness so that it could be absorbed and transmuted.

And my life's work made sense too! There in my genetics was the 48th Gene Key. The deep, dark well that keeps you in the fear of death until you are ready to face your own demons. When you do, you come up out of the well with answers and have the gift of Resourcefulness. I had certainly been resourceful each time I had dared to face my own demons. And at the Siddhic level of mastery, was Wisdom. The thing I had prayed for as a little girl was actually part of my DNA. I just needed to learn how to raise my Shadow vibration high enough to get there, which meant facing and embracing them. Most of those lessons for me were about learning to overcome my fear of not being enough and learning to love myself.

We can all reclaim our oneness and power as Super Heroes with Source whenever we are ready. It simply means letting go of old teachings and believing the truth that we are loved, accepted, whole and complete just the way we are. We don't need fixing. We are each on our journey toward discovery of the next level of ourselves. T. Harv Eker, author of Secrets of The Millionaire Mind says, "Every Master was once a disaster!" That is a statement of profound truth. Masters have just been courageous enough to make the mistakes in order to get to the next level. We are all learning. Each journey is unique, and no journey is wrong. It is WE who have forgotten our connection and become lost within ourselves, responding to fears of being alone, separated and unwanted. Creator has not left us; we have left Creator! Our amnesia, forgetting completely that Creator is within us and we are powerful co-creators, is the basis of our lack of authenticity and that which causes fear. Yet, how can we possibly be authentic if we have amnesia? How can we be authentic if we've forgotten we are loved and one with the Divine? If we don't think we're connected to Creator, we create our lives as if we're not. Look around you and see the proof of your creation. This world is living very much in an inauthentic way, full of greed, envy, lust and power. It's only when we realize we have a choice to believe the truth of our Divine connection that we can create from a place of love rather than a place of fear. I will get to the how-to-s of going beyond fear shortly, but let's examine the root of fear first.

Most fears are triggered by external circumstances that bring up a feeling which was felt during a prior trauma or negative experience. Something triggers the fight or flight response in the amygdala portion of the brain. It's the animal side of us that feels alone and disconnected. Here's how it happens: First, we are triggered by a familiar feeling of danger, which may or may not be real. Even if the perceived threat is not really dangerous, it certainly seems real in our bodies. Our stomachs may tense up, we may sweat profusely, our mouths may get dry, we may pace, and we may even hit things or lash out. The fear is only an illusion; a replay of old reactions looping back around from prior trauma. An underlying thought (many times subconscious) names why we feel this way, and it is projected first inwardly and then can be projected outwardly at someone or something else. These underlying thoughts invoke our inner judge, and make us good or bad, right or wrong, and all things are black and white. This is a function of the mind. The mind is the master computer database that stores all experiences in your life. If it perceives a similar experience to any trauma you've ever experienced, it triggers your brain to tell you "danger", and your emotions signal you that something is terribly wrong. Fight or flight time!

In the place of terror there is no room for change. There is no room for new perception of how to get through it. When we are in the middle of trauma, we are triggered to react a certain way because of the story we have created around the initial trauma. This 'story' was created by our mind computers to protect us. It is based in illusion and is a recreation of our negative feelings. Our 'story' is not based in fact. In that moment, we might not even be aware of what we tell ourselves because it has become such a subconscious habit. We get lost in our story, and the story we have made up keeps us locked into fear and repeating the trauma. It's a never-ending cycle that makes us feel trapped.

Here's the good news. We can overcome our feelings and go beyond our traumas if we are willing to explore our reactions by examining our feelings and self-talk during a trauma. What we tell ourselves holds the keys to freedom, because they tell us where our inner child is hurt and wounded. Here are some examples of things we might say to ourselves subconsciously:

- I can't go on. I just want to die!
- I'm all alone!
- This person/place/thing will ruin me!
- I'm not good enough.
- If he/she loved me they wouldn't do this
- I'm not lovable. (I'm ugly, fat, old, etc.)
- Nobody cares.
- I don't fit in.
- I don't deserve this.

According to the positive psychology movement, the trauma or negative experience imprints in the brain and creates a loop. This loop gets triggered by external events, and we are off and running in a pattern of negative self-talk with our subconscious mind controlling us from this old tape that is playing a story rather than fact. That imprint will be there forever, until it is recognized as a story or illusion and a new and stronger loop is created in the positive that can override it. Imagine it is like a cassette tape that has recorded a trauma, and in order to overcome it you must record a new loop of positivity. Both loops will exist simultaneously in your brain. The one that gets the most focus will be the one that becomes embodied. The old loop of reaction will soon give way to the new loop of positive focus and action. I include positive action, because we can't embody the new belief system until we act upon it. Because the imprint of the trauma has been looping as habit, we must focus on the new imprint for at least 21 days before our positive imprint will be able to overcome the old, negative imprint on the tape. This is scientific fact from brain science.

Let me give you an example from personal experience. When I was a little girl, my parents insisted that I eat shrimp cocktail. When I ate it, after begging my parents not to make me, I got violently ill because of an allergic reaction. Thereafter, I would never eat fish of any kind. When anyone ate fish, I would have to leave the building so I didn't vomit. I avoided harbors where they were cleaning fish so I didn't vomit from the smell. I avoided seafood restaurants because of the smell. The experience of being made to eat something I was allergic to caused repeated trauma for me. I created a belief system that I cannot eat seafood, although allergy testing showed me allergic to only certain kinds. The trauma from that single event as a child caused me so much pain that I couldn't bear repeating it and went deeply into subconscious fear. In that fear, I chose to avoid any connection to seafood for more than 30 years! That is a perfect example of where a response pattern was developed and continued to loop. Later in life, I sought assistance to clear this negative belief system, and now can successfully eat shrimp and lobster cooked in certain ways. I haven't cleared all of it, but I have dramatically improved. I can be on a wharf or have people eat seafood without gagging or feeling nauseated. I can order chicken in a seafood restaurant and enjoy others enjoying their seafood. I have unlocked some of the old patterns associated with my emotional, psychological and physical trauma that was caused when I ate shrimp as a little girl. Traumas can have mental, emotional and physical components, and all three must be cleared. Allergies can be a key indicator, because your physical body is screaming "No!" because of something it perceives as a danger. The body is intelligent. We need to learn to be more in touch with its wisdom!

So what was authentic truth and what was the story I created? I was being authentic when I told my parents I couldn't eat shrimp. In fact, it poisoned me. I have no idea how I knew, I just knew! However, the story I made up after that poisoning was based in fear of being poisoned again, fear of being forced to do something I didn't want to do, and fear of recreating the vomiting caused by eating the shrimp. My fear of seafood was so strong that when my kids were growing up they only ate fish and tuna sandwiches at their friends' houses. They never got it in my house because I couldn't open a can of tuna or smell fish without throwing up! Because I chose for many years to listen to and believe an old story that I had made up as a little girl, my trauma eventually affected another generation!

Another huge block to authenticity is denial of emotion. When we deny our fear, many times it is because we have grown accustomed to numbing out. If we numb out, we don't have to feel any negative emotions, and can act as if everything is alright and we are in control. One of the first places I look, as a spiritual guide, is whether or not this person is in touch with what they feel. I'm surprised, at times, that people can be raging, red-faced with veins popping in their necks, and are still saying everything is fine and nothing is going on with them! This is the proverbial elephant in the room. For those of you who think you can mask your emotions, think again. Regardless of how stoic and disconnected you've become to your own feelings, everyone else can feel them just by being near you. Your vibrations precede you! Remember the sixties, when we used to say, "I feel your vibe, man." There was more truth in that than anyone realized. Here's what a colleague, Dr. Sue Morter has to say about vibration:

> "We are made of Sound Vibration and Light. Underneath it all and behind that freshly shaven or coiffed and newly made-up face, there is an energy that cannot and will not be hidden. At least, not forever. Perhaps for now you are doing well to suppress, compress or depress. But your days are numbered. Eventually the Real You shines through. If you let it out soon enough, it comes with Grace and ease; if you are tough and can 'take the heat' and hold it in for quite some time, it could get ugly. It may have to burst out like a cannon…(sound familiar?! Oh that's what that noise was…).
>
> That energy moves in the form of a wave, like a musical score. It is comprised of all of the spoken and unspoken thoughts and feelings that you have. All the good stuff and all the…colorful stuff combined.
>
> You can assess its content by noticing what kinds of words and thoughts move through you each moment, and what kind of knots are in your stomach."

Our vibrations are emitted at all times, and they extend out sometimes 10 to 15 feet or more! While we may think we can hide our feelings, we can't. The world around us becomes our own personal mirror! Do you want to know what you really feel? If you're not sure, ask someone close to you. They feel your vibration and, if they feel safe enough to tell you, they will answer honestly.

Many times, people like to solicit counsel from people who will tell them what they want to hear, but when we do that, we continue in the denial. Ask someone you know loves you enough to be honest with you! And believe that your vibration, the essence of what you are 'being' in any given moment, may be completely different than what you think! This is "The Me I Couldn't See". I selected that title because we all have blind spots. Having people who love us enough to reflect back what we are really doing energetically is how we find these blind spots so we can go beyond them. If we continue in denial, it can keep us stuck in an illusion and can push away love. If we value authenticity in our lives, we need to know what we are really doing, even that which we cannot see!

It took me years to overcome my story and to understand how I was out of alignment with myself. As Dr. Sue Morter says, "...it can come bursting through like a cannon, and then it may not be so pleasant!" I definitely had a lot of cannons in my life! It doesn't have to be that way. You can overcome negative imprints quickly and easily with coaching and persistence, and guess what? You'll be on the path to the authentic you! Once you become aligned to your true self, capable of owning your blind spots and seeking truth, you begin to co-create your life with love and positivity, and the world mirrors it all right back at you!

CHAPTER 24

FINDING YOUR INNER VOICE

"Don't let the noise of others' opinions drown out your own inner voice."

- Steve Jobs

There are two inner voices. One is the ego voice, which I like to call our inner child. It is demanding. It is a taskmaster. Its purpose is to stay in control and keep us safe from anything that is perceived as dangerous. Of course, anything that asks us to surrender control, in the perception of the ego, is dangerous and vulnerable. This is why we are stuck in the illusion. We listen to this voice, and it is our worst critic! It could tell us we're bad, we're ugly, we're not good enough, and we'll never be good enough, or contrarily, it could tell us we're too good, and don't need anyone. This voice is connected to our human ego. It's not all bad. Consider it your inner child, who kept you alive all these years. This voice has served you well! You are simply now ready to go beyond it, into adulthood. The pain and anguish, the manipulations for control all come from that inner child who is trying to keep you safe! It was our survival mechanism as kids, and our inner child did his/her job perfectly. We made it through.

Now, though, it's time for the inner child to grow up and reach his/her potential. Does it make sense to live from the wounds of the little child, being told what to do from our human mind-computers that are capable only of rehashing old experiences? Of course not; we must allow the inner child to feel loved enough to let go so it doesn't wreak havoc in our lives. Once the inner child feels safe, then our adult self can find peace and reconnection with our Divine self!

The voice of your Divine self is pure and always wants what is best for you. It never judges you harshly yet is completely honest. It is objective and guides you toward truth and love. The Divine inner voice always considers what is right for you in every situation and assists in your spiritual growth and the growth of character. It also guides you into correct responses to others, regardless of how they act.

Finding your true inner voice isn't that hard. Meditation and calming the mind (which is the source of your ego) is the key. One of the best ways to begin to meditate is through guided meditation with someone who can hold the vibration high enough for you so you can let go of your mind and focus on the experience in the present tense. By letting yourself relax completely, your mind will start to chatter like a magpie! Don't worry; it is part of the process of becoming aware. Don't react to it, but simply choose to let the thoughts and chatter go in one ear and out the other. Simply let them pass through! The more you practice closing your eyes, opening your heart, and listening to your breathing, the faster you will be able to quiet your mind. It takes practice, but it is worth it. There are thousands of studies in the medical field that have proven that meditation improves all functions, including heart rate, blood pressure, emotions, and more. It is a key to peace and happiness. Don't give up after just a couple of tries. Let yourself experience whatever your body has to go through in order to relax. You'll find that once you are able to tune into your breathing and really feel your body, you will begin to open and experience light and love in your heart. It is a profound event.

One of my special gifts is the ability to bring forth the energy of Divine Love and hold it in the room for all people to feel and experience.

It dramatically changes lives. It wasn't a gift that came easily, as it took many years of deep meditation and study, clearing and working on myself. I needed to learn how to feel unconditionally loved by Creator so I could forgive myself. It is virtually impossible to love someone else unconditionally before we know the love of our Creator, and even then, we will go in and out of that love. We can't hold a consistent vibration of unconditional love at all times because of our humanness. But we can open to the Divine Love energy as much as possible, let it encircle us, empower us, and emanate through us. The more we feel it, the more tuned into it we are. That's why having someone who can transmit the light and vibration for you will assist you in learning how to develop this skill yourself. In the meantime, find someone more advanced than you, and allow them to help you. There are many people who offer guided meditations. Find someone you feel comfortable with and seek out Master Teachers you trust.

In the beginning, you won't be clear on which voice you are hearing. That's perfectly normal. It is very easy to think the ego voice is your higher self. It can fool us! That's why it is important to have someone more advanced who can see what you are doing and correct your way of thinking. Remember, our thinking is what we manifest. With incorrect thinking, we manifest things that may not be good for us!

Let's get clear about the ego voice that comes from the mind. It can bring us clear advice, too. Many millionaires are very much in their ego selves, yet they have learned the art of making money because they have implemented divine principles in dealing with money. They know self-discipline. They practice self-control, in many cases. What to watch for is how they treat the people around them. How is their life measuring up in other areas? Are they balanced? Are they respected? Are they honorable? Usually, people can have success in certain areas (like finances) but their lives are out of whack in other areas (like intimate relationships). Celebrities are perfect examples. I'm sure we can all name a few who have achieved phenomenal success, wealth and notoriety, yet have failed marriages and home lives. Many times, they are jumping from partner to partner, with a string of children behind them, with horror stories in the tabloids. None of us has every area of life mastered! In our humanness, we mistake power for divinity. This is something I'm still working on in my own life. One of my life lessons is learning to understand that difference. I'm sure many women can relate to this misunderstanding. We seek out strong masculine figures, seeing their strength of personality (ego), and then often realize that spiritually they are very weak.

The most important part of finding your inner voice is LISTENING. Be in silence. You can't hear the inner voice if you are constantly talking! True listening is an art. When we listen, it says we deeply care. When we really listen, we ignite understanding and compassion beyond the words. We can feel the vibration of the words. Listening to yourself, and discerning whether you are hearing the ego voice or the divine voice within may be the most profound thing you will ever do in your life!

CHAPTER 25

HOW DO I REMOVE MY BLOCKS?

"We all wear masks, and the time comes when we cannot remove them without removing some of our own skin."

- André Berthiaume

The most effective way to remove blocks is to do personal inner work. By inner work, I mean going into deep meditation and listening to your inner voice. That voice will guide you and let you know your state of being. For example, in my quest for healing, I decided it was time to clear my old "story" about seafood. In order to clear my pattern, I went deeply into the emotional experience of my trauma. I closed my eyes, recalling the incident as a little girl. I began to name my feelings. As I watched the movie of me in my head, my feelings and self-talk went something like this:

I am angry at my parents for making me eat shrimp. I am feeling overpowered and forced against my will. It's not fair. I am nauseous. I am vomiting. I am violently ill. I am breaking out in hives. I am in a cold sweat. I am running a fever. I am screaming "I told you so, but you wouldn't listen". Then it begins to escalate into "Nobody listens to me! Nobody cares what I think! You don't love me! You're trying to kill me! Seafood will kill me! I can't eat seafood. I will never eat seafood again! You can't make me!"

As I uncovered my little girl's reaction, I found the subconscious story I had made up. Nobody listens and nobody cares. Nobody loves me. I am not seen and heard. I don't count. People are trying to kill me. I will die before I eat seafood again. Now, are these statements truth? Of course not! They were the "story" I created in my little girl feelings because of the imprint of the negative experience. This is that Shadow of Inadequacy and Fear of Death I was talking about in my DNA. From that story, I created a belief system that told me never to eat seafood or I would die. Did my parents care? Of course, my parents cared! They weren't trying to kill me! They were simply doing what they thought was best by making me eat seafood. It was logical from a parental perspective. Seafood is healthy and therefore I should make my kid try it! They felt terrible after I got sick. Unfortunately, I continued in the pattern of nobody listens to me, I don't count, and people are trying to kill me for years. As I analyzed it, it seemed to be a recurring story that was looping in many of the traumas in my life.

Once you've gone deeply into feeling the experience (which, I might add, can be very painful, but necessary in order to clear it out of your body), and you've identified the stories you told yourself about the experience, they are brought into your conscious mind to clear. To go beyond it, it's necessary to create positive declarations about yourself and repeat them until the positive loop becomes the dominant pattern. Mine were, "I am listened to and respected. I am loved. I count. I make my own decisions in life. Seafood won't kill me. The smell of seafood doesn't make me sick. I'm ready now to go beyond the trauma of my little girl experience and take back control of my life." Making these declarations out loud solidifies them in the conscious mind. The spoken word is connected to our patterning, just as the old self talk is. Understand that the goal was not to be able to eat something that I was allergic to, but to clear the negative belief system around the trauma experience. For me, however, it was an added bonus to be able to begin eating shrimp slowly, as it was proof to me that I had actually cleared a lot of trauma. The deeper issues, of course, were not feeling loved, feeling overpowered, and not being respected. Again, I found these were recurring patterns for me. And to think, this was all triggered (not caused) by one little incident where my parents wanted me to try a particular food. It is sometimes so innocent. Parents want to do their best with their children, but no parent is perfect and we all have wounds from growing up.

It is important to take personal responsibility for ourselves in all things. There is no one to blame. Things happen. The truth is we can continue to perceive them as "bad and wrong" and we will never heal. It takes a willingness to go beyond judgment of others and look within ourselves to the truth of how we have created a "story" in order to be right about our feelings. We get so caught up in being right that we can't see our own story we've made up. If we're not honest with ourselves, we will continue projecting blame onto others and circumstances rather than allowing ourselves healing. It takes self-forgiveness and forgiveness of those who were involved. And guess what? It's worth it. You'll be amazed at how you begin to see how comical you have been in your stories, once you get beyond self- judgment. Listen, we all do it. We all have stories. We all have blind spots where we think we're right. It takes a big person to be willing to go deep and want to heal. I always ask my clients, "Do you want to be right or do you want to heal? Which is most important right now?" If you are at a place where you want to heal, then "Bravo". Go for it! If not, and you need to be right awhile longer, that's o.k. too. Be honest about it. Say to yourself, "I want to hang onto this pain a little longer. It serves me right now." Even though it sounds ridiculous that we choose to hold on to pain, that's exactly what we do! It's all our choice. Remember, you are the product of many years of teachings and it takes time to go beyond some of those teachings to find your own truth. It takes an admission that we don't know it all. It takes a surrendering of pride to say we've made a mistake. We have to be able to feel safe in order to go there.

My suggestion is to find someone who can be a non-judgmental coach for you in these areas. There are many professional coaches and guides who work in this way.

Remember, it's not your fault. Our parents, teachers and authority figures in this human realm have taught us that we must do things a certain way; a way that is driven by the human ego, and completely foreign to the truth of who we are. It's not their fault, either! Every generation has done the best it could based on what they knew. Thank goodness we are now coming back into awakening to the truth. For many thousands of years, however, humankind has believed that we must perform certain ways to be accepted and loved. Here are just a few of the subconscious belief systems we have created, along with the implied fear statement in italics. You might recognize some of them in your own belief system:

- We must get an education and/or job *or we'll never amount to anything.*
- Money is the key to happiness. *If we don't have it we can't be happy.*
- Showing emotion lacks wisdom and leaves us vulnerable, *and if we're vulnerable, people will take advantage of us.*
- Things must be logical and explainable in physical reality *or they aren't real.*
- Money is the root of all evil. *If I have money, I am evil.*
- I must earn love. *Love is only given when I perform.*
- Life is hard. *And then you die.*

These are just a few of the misguided teachings many of us have accepted into our subconscious minds as truth. However, in reality, there are thousands, maybe even millions of un-truths embedded in our subconscious minds, all based in fear.

Just look at the advertising industry. We are subjected to fear-based advertising every minute, getting over 400,000 impressions a day that all say, "Buy this or you won't be sexy! Buy that or you won't fit in". Of course, it's all very subtle and we don't even realize the messages we are taking in on a subconscious level. It's really quite insidious. Beautiful models in magazines that are air brushed, free of all blemishes, shining in their radiance with perfect bodies are not real! Yet this is what our teenage girls have as role models of the "norm" for beauty; what they are subconsciously told they are supposed to look like. It's not only inauthentic, it's outright deceptive to get us to buy the product they are selling. The deeper, more insidious message is that we're not good enough the way we are, and we'll only get love and be successful if we look like these models. What a sad message to deliver to our impressionable youth. It sets them up to feel inferior for life, and approach the rest of their lives in fear that someone else will get the job, the guy, etc. because they will never look that way.

When I was working on a radio show a number of years ago, I hosted a gentleman who had made a documentary film on a 12-year old girl who had "hit the big time" as a supermodel in New York. Mind you, it was against the law for runway models to be that young, but did that stop the powers that be? She was "talented"! And her talent? She could dress up in sexy clothing and shoes, wear high fashion make up, and sell the crowd that she was 22 and sexy, with lots of life experience. She had it all, she thought; magazine and television interviews, the hottest fashions, money and success. She was at the beginning of a huge international career, until she turned 14 and grew to be a size 3. She was told after less than 2 years, she was "too big" for the clothing and was treated as if she was yesterday's news. When I did the interview, this young girl had gone through tremendous pain and suffering, feeling like she was fat and ugly. One minute she was a supermodel, the next she was nothing. She felt like she no longer had an identity. It took several years for her to pull herself back together and find enough self-esteem to go back to high school. You can imagine the comments from her peers. They were jealous when she had it all, and scoffing at her when she returned with nothing. There was no compassion. Was it fair? NO! This poor young girl was taught by her mother and by society that if she was inauthentic and played a role she would be famous. The truth about things that are not authentic is that they never last.

What about raising our children to believe they are beautiful just the way they are, at their age, at their weight, at their height, with all their seeming imperfections? When will we learn as parents that it's not our job to make our kids "acceptable" to the world's rules, but rather to teach them to be successful at loving and accepting themselves and being authentic? If this girl's mother believed that, I doubt she would have ever put her into the modeling world to get crushed. Sadly, at the time of the interview, it appeared Mom was still looking for ways to make her daughter famous. It seemed to be all about money, attention and power. That's not love, and yet this mother thought she was doing the right thing by her daughter because her daughter loved modeling.

Sometimes, our lives give us no choice but to learn and grow. Sixteen years ago, when I was diagnosed with six months to live by numerous doctors, rather than having my entire large intestine surgically removed, I chose to investigate how I had gotten into such a mess, and to work with Creator and a natural healer to bring myself back to health. I made the decision that it just wasn't my time to check out. It took 2 years of intense therapy, and lots of hard work on my part, but I made it through. My health is amazing today, and I look ten years younger than I did 10 years ago! I attribute my complete healing to being open to experience truth and healing any way I needed to. It included healing my mind, emotions, physical body and spirit.

It was during that process, that one of my doctors talked to me about psychic pain. I sought a past life regression specialist, which was something I had never done before and didn't even know if it was something I believed in, but I gave it a try. I uncovered lifetime after lifetime of being killed, and one particular lifetime where I had been stabbed repeatedly and was disemboweled after being attacked in a dark alley in Italy. Was it true? Who knows? But really, who cares? My health after that session took an amazing leap, after I was able to let go of the pain and trauma from my body. I also found it interesting that there was so much emotion during the remembrance of these other lifetimes. I was sobbing uncontrollably over many of them, experiencing the pain as if it were happening in the present tense. When I was done, I asked myself if I believed all I had been through. While admittedly, it was nothing I could prove, I believed I had some sort of cleansing experience that helped me deeply. And Creator knows I couldn't have made up the stories about those lifetimes. They were just too detailed and full of emotion!

Before we learn and completely understand the truth about clearing blocks that hinder our authentic selves, it might feel like the world is against us and we might begin to question where Creator is in it all. I certainly did, when faced with death. It's normal. Again, I say to you, that it is YOU who is at the helm, bringing up these events so that you can be cleared of pain and fear. Being a healing investigator, you can try it all. You're so smart! Look how much you want to heal yourself!

CHAPTER 26

HUMAN GUIDES & HEALERS

"No man is great enough or wise enough for any of us to surrender our destiny to. The only way in which anyone can lead us is to restore to us the belief in our own guidance."

- Henry Miller

In order for anyone to understand themselves and change their subconscious belief systems, a human spiritual guide may be needed to assist with changing old patterns and transmuting old, negative energies and belief systems. A Master Teacher or Spiritual Healer/ Guide who has gone through the process of awakening themselves to their own authenticity, can skillfully and lovingly question possible ego issues, while holding the energy of love, acceptance, understanding and compassion when mistakes are made. They understand that it is simply a part of the process of the evolution of spirit. This human guide should exhibit certain character qualities, and I have outlined 10 which I think are highly important. Make sure your human guide has a number of these qualities, before you work with them over the long term. Not everyone will exhibit all 10, but without at least 5 or 6, I'd say move on to someone else! You may also find, as I did, that you may want to work with different Masters at different times, because they each have a unique gift to bring to your development at certain points in time. Avoid at all costs, the "guru" who doesn't want you to study with others or attend other spiritual events. A great Master Teacher should be able to guide you to your own mastery, rather than keeping you as a student, and while they should be paid for their work, money should not be their primary motivation. Keep this in mind in the overall evaluation. I always like it when Master Teachers have other businesses or skills for which they make money in the world. That tells me they can be truly heart centered and not motivated from survival.

Here are the 10 qualities of a Master Teacher or Spiritual Guide (not necessarily in order of importance):

1) Humility (Letting you find your answers from within yourself)
2) Peace (Confident and detached from your choices)
3) Patience (Not expecting results in their timing but in yours)
4) Can Manifest Their Own Worldly Needs (Not destitute!)
5) Wisdom and Clarity of Thought (Psychic perception & Advice)
6) Love and Acceptance, with psychic gifts connected to Spirit (clairaudience, clairvoyance, clairsentience, etc.)
7) Understanding and Compassion (Your biggest cheerleader)
8) Strength and Courage To Stand Alone (Not afraid to speak truth)
9) A Continual Learner (Knowing they don't have all the answers)
10) Respect for Earth and an Understanding of Oneness with All (Seeing all things as connected, especially you and them!)

Opening to new awareness of our spirit is the same as riding a bicycle. When we first began to learn how to pedal, we needed someone to come along side us and hold us up. As we learn how to connect to our authentic spiritual selves, we need a guide to "hook us up" into the aligned energy of the spiritual realm. The guide acts as a conduit or bridge, helping you connect to other dimensions, acting also as a beacon of light; hearing, seeing and feeling the other side and reflecting it back for you until you can hear and see and feel it yourself. The rate of growth for each of us is up to each and every individual. Some move very rapidly, as I did. Others choose to move more slowly and with caution. There is no right or wrong way, and your journey is your journey and cannot be judged by any other human. It is between you and Creator. I work at practicing the art of allowing people to be where they are, (ACCEPTANCE-the hardest lesson of all) and it makes for a very successful healing session. When I do, my ego is out of the way with no judgment or expectation. This is the goal of every coach or spiritual guide. It's not always easy! I want people to get it immediately and quickly!

Many of you have heard about the Law of Attraction. If we are allowing the filter of negative events and feelings in our lives to run us by subconscious default then what do we get back? Negative events! My experiences are a perfect example of the subconscious drift. I allowed my subconscious patterns of fear and rejection to live out to the point of near death, as I described in previous chapters.

Taking the journey of authenticity corrects the subconscious drift. When we feel safe enough to look at ourselves honestly, we are admitting before Creator where we are out of synch, where we are wounded and blind, and then we can learn what we need to begin healing ourselves. By going beyond self-judgment, realizing that we are designed to be human and make mistakes, so we can learn and evolve, then we can live a life of freedom and peace. We can accept that we each have a dark side or ego side and laugh; accepting it rather than following it. Mistakes are no longer deadly sins, and we are not afraid of being damned for eternity for not being perfect. Our definition of perfection is not the same definition as Creator's. In Creator's eyes we are already perfect in our humanness. When we stumble and learn lessons, it was by His design that we reach for reconnection to the part of us that is connected to eternity so that we can become one with His mind and heart. As we open to spiritual healing by becoming a logical observer of ourselves without judgment, we automatically become more authentic and more Creator-like. We release negative patterns and open to new illumination and so we can create new, positive patterns with conscious intent. This is the realm of new possibilities, and it is infinite! There is nothing that is too bad, too dark, or too hard to overcome. It is ALL GOOD, when we can perceive it as a journey and move to a higher level of consciousness.

The Secret was a great movie that got out the message that we create our reality through our thoughts. The problem was that it didn't go deeply enough into the truth of what is required for conscious co-creation through our authentic natures. We can't simply think about money and write checks and have money show up! We got in the debt mess we are in by acting on our faulty belief system. It was made evident right before our eyes! We can't change our circumstances through declaring it to be so, although positive thinking and declarations are part of the equation. We must all work at being authentic, which means we are willing to investigate the light and dark within ourselves and adjust our actions and habits accordingly, bringing everything into balance. We must realize that we are acting subconsciously on old belief patterns and training. If we are not doing these things consciously, conscious declarations won't change a thing. We need to have a deep awareness of our subconscious belief system to be able to consciously create something new. It takes work. It takes thought. It takes a willingness to be honest about our feelings and habits. As we live and experience this awareness, we become more authentic, we live a more balanced life, and we attract that which we want into our lives in order to manifest the things we care about and choose to create. If we are making positive declarations but haven't cleared out the subconscious debris, we may still be drawing in that which we don't want!

Becoming authentic takes a willingness to commit to being open and honest enough with ourselves that we can discover the beauty and power of who we are as spiritual beings, forgive ourselves for our mistakes, and admit and overcome our blind spots. Authenticity requires complete transparency and openness to being held accountable. People on an authentic path seek other people to assist them to understand their blind spots. Through facing our blind spots, we are able to clear and grow, and ultimately make the changes that will bring about the desired result in our lives.

When was the last time you pictured yourself naked before Creator? It takes humility and transparency. Nothing can be hidden; not our feelings (positive and negative) our perceptions, or our judgments. It's all presented before Creator in honesty and integrity. The joke is, Creator already sees it anyway! Who are we kidding?

This journey also involves a constant choice to be responsible for our own feelings and actions. No one and no thing are causing you pain. Obstacles will come. Heartbreak will come. But the way we respond to them is written through our subconscious belief systems. If we don't take full responsibility for our feelings and behavior, we project things onto others and stay completely locked in the victim mode. By choosing to be responsible for ourselves in all things, we grow our consciousness in a positive way. This very simple truth created the new coaching/ positive psychology movement in our world today. It is looking at the positive possibilities and focusing on what we want rather than what is. In doing so, we create new solutions to old problems.

CHAPTER 27

LETTING GO OF OLD WAYS AND PEOPLE WE'VE OUTGROWN

"Some people are like clouds. When they disappear, it becomes a beautiful day."

- Unknown

One of the toughest parts of the journey toward authenticity is realizing that sometimes you have to stand alone with Creator. Once you are well on your path to healing and are feeling and experiencing your connection of love and the ability to create your reality, you realize that as you grow and change, the people in your world don't necessarily grow with you. This is probably the most painful part of growth. The more authentic I become, the less I have in common with old friends and acquaintances and the more I long for my one-on-one relationship with Creator and other people who have the same understanding of that relationship. It's not your friends and family who have changed; it's YOU who have changed! When you find yourself in this place where you don't feel like you connect with your old friends and peer group, know that you are in the middle of a major shift. You have let go of the old and must trust that the new just hasn't yet appeared. This is where our faith produces endurance. If we wait, we will see that which is new and perfect. We must learn to allow the spaces in between. These spaces strengthen our faith and are useful in spiritual development.

Another area that might change might be within your intimate family. We are all born into families we have chosen, and these are the people who we typically have the most to work out. We are guided to a certain religious group or lineage simply because we're born into it. This isn't a bad thing. We can be devoted to Creator wherever we are. It all counts! When you begin growing spiritually and making changes in your life, you'll find old friends and family aren't amenable to your changes. They want you to stay where you are. Human stasis is predominant. We just don't like change!

A very close friend of mine told me a story one time about the crab in the box that helped me a lot. I was working very hard on myself and my friends and family began making fun of my new level of spirituality and exploration. It was tough. Some of them even got nasty and told me I had forgotten my roots and was now not practicing true love for Creator. That hurt! I was doing just that, but my friends and family couldn't see it. My friend shared a story that I often repeat to my clients. Mind you, fishermen know about this, but maybe because of my aversion to seafood, I had never heard it!

> A box of crabs was pulled up from their crab cages and put on the wharf. These crabs knew they were trapped, and were diligently trying to get out. One crab hooked one of his legs on the top of the box. He had enough strength and initiative to make it to the top of the box and was just about ready to tip over the side to freedom. Just then, another crab hooked a leg onto his lower leg and pulled him back down into the box. Instead of working together to help the crab become free, it was all about keeping him stuck in the status quo. If I'm in here, you have to be here too!

That's exactly what we do to each other as human beings. When someone is rising up on a new path toward freedom, many times we kick them in the shins and tell them it won't work, and even worse, seek to hold them back. Rather than supporting their effort to find truth, we make them bad and wrong. After all, they aren't staying within the status quo. It takes courage to stand up and be who you are. It takes guts to make it to the top of the box. Don't let any crabs pull you back down. Simply let them go and don't get hooked by their remarks and kicks!

What is sad is that many religious leaders still don't get that fact. Have you noticed that many, in fact the majority of religions, say they're the best? They each represent they have the real answers and know Creator like other religions don't. While it is true that each religion holds a unique perspective and energy in the Creator relationship, the truth is not in exclusion, dogma and spiritual traditions! This is a perfect example of leaders who have been taught a certain way and who are passing it on as absolute truth, rather than opening up to the fact that as humans we only see bits and pieces of Creator. We are constantly growing and learning from our own experiences and taking into consideration the experiences, thoughts and feelings of others. We were meant to evolve into our authentic, divine selves. The person who doesn't readily accept this as truth is the person who plays the fool. Once we, as human beings, think we know it all and try to make others believe the way we do, we are playing Creator, not serving Creator. While this may sound harsh, let me say that every human being goes through this stage of growth. We all play Creator in certain ways. Having to be right about our belief system is one of them. It's born out of a power and control model. I know this truth and you don't. I'm superior to you. Yet, all the truly enlightened beings who ever walked Earth shared that the closer they got to Creator, the more they realized how little they knew, and the more compassion they found for their fellow man! That is truth and is authentic. The question we need to ask is **not,** "Is my religion the right or best religion?" May I suggest that the question we should be asking today is, "How am I becoming my authentic self and making the world a better place?" Authenticity goes beyond the boundaries of religion to pure, unadulterated spirituality; our pure selves in spiritual form.

We, as a world, are now awakening to the new reality that is present that goes beyond our own exclusive religions. We now have the ability to become leaders in an entirely new way. We can accept our brothers and sisters wherever they are and find compassion. We can work together toward love, rather than toward being right, or having power and control over others.

When we let go of having to be right and allow ourselves to be on our chosen path and everyone else on theirs, we lose our self-righteous attitudes toward others and can meet them in love, compassion and peace.

The sad thing about religion is that many leaders have become spiritualized egos, rather than enlightened beings. Many think they are operating in their higher self, but their egos are actually running the show. Having to be right is a function of ego. If we look at all the religions, we will find NO EXCEPTIONS. The most horrendous atrocities have been committed in the name of Creator! The Catholics have more wealth than most countries combined. They have also allowed pedophilia in the church hierarchy. Some Christian fundamentalists fight for the rights of children not to be aborted, saying they are preventing murder, and then bomb doctors' clinics, killing all those inside. Radical Islam claims Jihad against capitalism and western carnal living, and yet murdered hundreds of people during 911, while its leaders participated in pornography and terror. Some Jewish leaders claim the right to bomb Palestine because they are the chosen people and have a right to their land. Some Palestinians bomb Israel because they say their people have a right to live where they want. Get the picture? Religions claim to have the answers from Creator but have forgotten that oneness, love and compassion is Creator's #1 standard of measure. When religious leaders begin being authentic and begin to do their own inner work before Creator, letting go of their own pain and trauma and self- judgment and self-righteousness, then and only then will we begin to come together in peaceful coexistence with our brothers and sisters of other races and religions. We don't all need to believe one way about Creator. Our diverse backgrounds give us pieces of information about all that Creator is, if we would simply look at it that way! It's time to look at the similarities we have as humans, rather than allowing our diversities to separate us. Our authentic selves are much bigger than that.

I've also come to believe that we have unconscious fear patterns that are embedded in cell memory beyond this lifetime, and much of that is carried in our lineage though our DNA. It makes sense that we, as eternal spirits, incarnate into a physical body over and over again in order to mature ourselves. We are bound to have unresolved traumas that are carried from lifetime to lifetime either through prior incarnations or through our Ancestral DNA. Hypnosis is especially effective to assist us to find these traumas and relieve them from our psyches. I utilize past life regression with my clients, and it is amazing the lifetimes that come springing forth ready to clear. I've had other therapists use those techniques with me, and the energies through that work allowed me to overcome something from my ancestral DNA that was being triggered by current events. If you have been taught that reincarnation is the devil, before you throw this book, perhaps you might want to look into why you fear that as truth. Isn't reincarnation simply the law of reaping what you sow? It is the energy of our actions that outlives us, and these energies need to be cleared. Call it past lives, karma, ancestral fear, whatever you like. But don't make it bad and wrong. When we do, it is a classic example of being taught something and then having to be right about it. It's akin to Galileo being imprisoned by the church because he said the earth revolved around the sun, rather than vice versa. It wasn't the acceptable belief of the time, but later came to be proven as truth. Perhaps this might be one where you want to open to experience rather than judge. Besides, what harm does it cause to have an experience that might teach us something new? You don't open yourself to darkness by trying to heal; you open yourself to darkness by staying in fear of the darkness!

In order to become world leaders, we must be willing to go on a journey for a number of years to clear pain and trauma and evaluate our belief systems. If there are people in your life who don't understand and support you on your quest, then let them go. Politely hold a boundary for yourself. If everyone in the world decided to work on this journey of authenticity, just think what the world would be like! Think what could be accomplished!

CHAPTER 28

HEAD VS. HEART

"Your heart knows things that your mind can't explain."

- KushandWizdom

I decided I would devote an entire chapter to the difference between living from your head vs. your heart. When I talk about the "head", I'm actually talking about the mind, or the ego-self. While it is true that we have a "higher mind", that "higher mind" is actually guidance from the heart. So just for the purpose of explanation and to be clear, the head or the mind is our computer that processes all of the experiences we have ever had as human beings. It holds the essence of our personality, too. The mind is very powerful, and what we see in each other is the expression of the mind and personality. This is complete with subconscious pain, wounding and trauma from this lifetime, from previous lifetimes, and from our lineage.

The heart space, or the Divine connection to Source, is the true authentic you that is your real driver, once it is awakened. Picture yourself in a limousine. The car itself is your physical body. Your Divine Self is in the Driver's seat, driving you exactly according to plan, unless the backseat driver (your mind-ego-personality) overrides it and tells it what to do!

Think about how silly we are! We allow our ego personalities to tell our Spirit (driver) what to do, when our Spirit (driver) knows best. After all, he/she is being guided by the best... Creator!

The journey of this lifetime is to learn to sit back and let your Spirit drive the car. Bind and gag the personality in the back seat if you have to, because all he knows is what he has experienced, and he will keep leading you in a vicious circle. If the definition of insanity, according to Albert Einstein, is doing the same thing over and over and expecting different results, then why do we want the mind or personality-self to lead? And yet, that is the human condition. We mistrust. We want control. We want power. And look where it has gotten us.

My mission during this lifetime is to bring in streams of love energy to the planet. I'm here to shine a light for people to know their path. Once people feel loved and see their path, they can begin to let go and not feel that they have to fight for their survival. I have the ability to call in light energy beyond my own physical body and connect my clients into that bio-energetic matrix, which allows healing beyond traditional methods. Some of this might sound pretty far out, but you can't argue with success. My clients, family and friends are a testament to the fact that it works. I'm no one special. I'm simply a woman who has been open to Creator Source and the spiritual realms of light and love. Each and every one of you reading this book has unique gifts and abilities that are waiting to manifest. All you need to do is to begin the path toward authenticity. Once you embark on that path, we can begin to work together, honoring the Earth and her resources, and honoring our fellow brothers and sisters. If there is one thing I've learned along the way, it is that it is up to each of us individually, and each of us is connected to all that exists. That means whatever I do today affects everyone on the planet, and whatever you do today affects me and everybody else on the planet too!

There are three different types of consciousness: The Individual Consciousness, The Collective Consciousness, and Creator

Consciousness. We work with all three types of consciousness and need to be clear that all three consciousness forms are operating at the same time, all interacting with one another. If the Individual Consciousness (our human part) isn't awakened to the other two, we can live life in a drift of subconscious creation from our wounded egos that manifests things we don't necessarily desire. When all three are consciously co-creating, life is magical and synergistic.

Going from your head or mind to your heart is the most important thing you will ever do in this lifetime. A couple of years ago, I had the privilege of attending a speaking engagement with Dr. Howard Martin, a VP at the HeartMath Institute. The mission of the Institute of HeartMath is to help establish heart-based living and global coherence by inspiring people to connect with the intelligence and guidance of their own hearts. It is interesting that HeartMath has taken a different approach than traditional science, determining that the heart and the brain intercommunicate.

> "Traditionally, the study of communication pathways between the "head" and heart has been approached from a rather one-sided perspective, with scientists focusing primarily on the heart's responses to the brain's commands. However, we have now learned that communication between the heart and brain is actually a dynamic, ongoing, two-way dialogue, with each organ continuously influencing the other's function. Research has shown that the heart communicates to the brain in four major ways: neurologically (through the transmission of nerve impulses), biochemically (via hormones and neurotransmitters), biophysically (through pressure waves) and energetically (through electromagnetic field interactions). Communication along all these conduits significantly affects the brain's activity. Moreover, our research shows that messages the heart sends the brain can also affect performance." http://www.heartmath.org/research/science-of-the-heart/head-heart-interactions.html

In a recent study, they found that the heart actually sends messages to the brain, and the brain synchronizes with the heart. When positive emotions are invoked, the brain's electrical activity becomes more synchronized during psychophysiologically coherent states. This implies that the heart may actually alter information in the brain during positive emotions.

> "In conclusion, this study shows that the brain's activity is naturally synchronized to that of the heart, and also confirms that intentionally altering one's emotional state through heart focus modifies afferent neurological input from the heart to the brain. Results indicate that the brain's electrical activity becomes more synchronized during psychophysiologically coherent states. Implications are that this increased synchronization may alter information processing by the brain during the experience of positive emotions."

> http://www.heartmath.org/research/science-of-the-heart/head-heart-interactions.html

In my work, I seek to assist people to come to grips with the fact that they are both the observer and the observed; the actor, the playwright and the audience in the drama of our lives. While most people think they are in their hearts, there is a very unique difference between how we feel about our opinions (emanating from our minds) and how we can tune into our hearts to raise our vibration and state of consciousness. My experience has shown me that when I am in a negative emotional state, my world around me collapses right along with me. When I am in a positive and joyous state, I am able to create with ease and manifest exactly what I want. One energetic vibration blocks positive manifestation, the other opens up to positive manifestation. Being in your heart is really the truth of who you are…. your authentic self. It is a crystal of truth that operates within you that is connected to the energy of Divine Creator Him/Herself!

So how can someone tell if they are in their mind or their heart? I find it interesting that most people I work with think they are in their heart but they are simply acting on the computer chip inside their brains. Here is one way to tell the difference. If you are constantly worrying about an issue and trying to resolve it, you are in your mind. You are operating like a computer processor would operate. Unfortunately, you cannot resolve it because the information in the processor is all old data from past experience. In order to really resolve an issue, you must breathe deep, rest the mind, and drop into your heart. Many people discover that meditation is the fastest way to drop into their hearts. It's all about calming the mind, thus shifting from the egoic state to the divine state. It takes practice. It doesn't happen overnight. I can tell you though, that once you begin a meditation practice, your life begins to rapidly change! You will instantly feel the benefits of calming the mind, and the listening to your inner guidance. It has always been there. Your mind has simply been too busy chatting away to allow you to hear it!

There are many meditations that will assist you to quiet your mind and open your heart. All you need to do is have the intention, take about 20 or 30 minutes, and relax. Let your mind go, relax your body and begin to feel your heart again. It may take some time before your mind will stop its incessant chatting. Don't worry! Let it do its thing and say, "Thank you for sharing!" If you ignore it and don't listen, it will eventually calm down. The more you focus on your heart and the feelings and sensations in your body, the more your heart will begin to open. You may even begin to see colors, which is a very good sign that there are energy streams opening up in your body. Enjoy the experience! There are hundreds of advantages to meditation, including your physical and mental health. Don't let anyone tell you it's stupid or time consuming. There is nothing that will advance you or energize you like meditation. Meditation is receiving from Creator. We have been trained to pray to Creator, but we have not learned how to properly receive. I'd say we are way out of balance, don't you think? How can we receive Creator's love when we are talking incessantly?

CHAPTER 29

BEGINNING THE JOURNEY

"I'm astounded by people who want to 'know' the universe when it's hard enough to find your way around Chinatown."

- Woody Allen

We can all appreciate Woody Allen's humor. Life is definitely a paradox. Yet, the good news is that we all have the guide map back to Creator within our hearts, so our journey isn't nearly as hard as we think. Our ultimate destination in any lifetime is to complete the circle, to return home to complete union with Creator. Before our human bodies die, we can accomplish this energetically. It is what many of the Masters that have walked the Earth have called 'enlightenment'. Everything you need for your journey you have already been given. It will be activated within you when you are ready to make a decision to reach for your authentic self.

The fundamental pattern that I will illustrate through my own life is so familiar that its basic theme can be found within the mythologies of virtually every culture in the world. Joseph Campbell investigated this pattern, called the Hero's Journey archetype, in his book, *A Hero with a Thousand Faces.* In this story, the hero must travel far from home to overcome many difficult obstacles. When he returns, he has achieved a higher state of being, having become a true hero in service to humanity.

No matter how difficult your life may seem, you may begin to regard yourself as a kind of hero. You may have traveled far away from who you really are, but you are destined to return home again. When you embark on your journey to return, you are on the path that reveals the truth of your authentic self. The journey is beautiful, and you will begin to understand and accept that you are much bigger, more beautiful and greater than you could ever have imagined. You carry the Creator spark within you!

Many of you may not have ever thought about this journey back home to Creator. We are so conditioned to perceive human life as all there is; a series of events and then we die. It may seem that our external circumstances have huge power over us, yet all the experiences have been uniquely guided by the inner you without your conscious awareness. There is no right or wrong in the facts of your life. They are all just neutral experiences created for you and by you for your own growth and healing. Your spirit is absolutely brilliant when it comes to growing you! Many will ask "How can experiences all be neutral when there is right and wrong?" My answer is that, of course, there is the ethical plane of existence, and we all get hurt and abused at different times in our lives. Yet these experiences all provide us opportunities to choose the way we will respond. By living the game of life as if you created everything in it, you can experience holding compassion and boundaries in a field of pure love that even transcends right and wrong.

You've heard of people who have gone through horrible experiences, and yet who grew beyond the pain to forgiveness and compassion. These people, instead of being victimized over and over again in their minds and hearts, have consciously chosen to focus on what they personally learned about themselves rather than the story they made up about the negative experience. They realized they couldn't change the facts of what happened, but they could change their own outlook on what happened. And it was in this new perception that they were able to release the toxic thinking and move forward as stronger and more compassionate individuals. They learned the art of focusing on and building their own character through the response of your higher self.

I am blessed with three daughters, who walked parts of my difficult journey right along with me. Now they are each working their own life path and in their own way bringing light into the world. They have given me six beautiful grandchildren who bring unending joy into my life. These little ones have become my best teachers, reflecting back to me the purity that exists at the core of the human heart and soul. Naturally wise, they are so full of life and light. They know nothing but love, constantly reminding me of my own pure, essential self.

I hope this book will take you back to enjoying yourself and who you are, as you realize that everything you have experienced is your own creation. While we don't necessarily consciously create the circumstances, we attract people and circumstances are created because we have something to learn. The divine spirit within us provides an opportunity to heal ourselves and go to the next level of authenticity. How you respond is what you are held accountable for and is what determines the outcome of events. You are only responsible for your part, not the responses of others. Learning to respond appropriately rather than react is essential to our growth into the authentic self.

Creating a new life begins with understanding the duality within each of us and through transforming habits and patterns. As we begin to become aware of "The Me I Couldn't See" both human and divine, we can consciously choose to transform our habits and patterns and become more resident in the authentic divine self. When we do reside in our authentic divine self, we automatically influence the world around us in a positive way.

Have you ever noticed that when you make positive changes in your life, the people around you see and comment on the changes? You begin to see that it is all worth it, and you feel free and empowered. Once you have made peace with yourself and all people in your life as much as it is within your capability to do so, you can learn how to go beyond transformation to transmutation. It is a shift from the control by the mind to the control center from within your heart. You become a light guide! Be forewarned, however that it is a path that takes patience and persistence, as well as time to allow growth and integration into your life. Ultimately, it's an eternal process of learning, and it is one that can bring great joy and satisfaction. This is the way of the alchemist, who transmutes the darkness into light; and who can turn the pain of life into absolute joy. It is the secret of living within your divine connection, your authentic self. You begin to live your "I AM" presence.

If the idea of being a light guide feels a little uncomfortable, don't worry. It's not about wearing tie-dye, collecting crystals, and smelling of patchouli. If any of those things assist you on your path, that's great. But in the end, being a light guide is about something far more real than any object to be found in the physical world. Becoming a light guide is a matter of moving out of the realm of the mind and into the space of the heart. A light guide is someone committed to knowing all facets of themselves deeply and authentically, beyond the facades of the ego or personality identity.

In the long run, I have found that no single religion or sacred text is capable of containing the entirety of Truth. And, like so many other human activities, religions can foster a great deal of spiritual judgment and can subtly nurture the seeds of darkness in the human soul, even while claiming to be its salvation. I still value the religious phase of my life very much and cherish all the spiritual knowledge I have gained in that phase of my growth. Since that time, however, Spirit has revealed Truth to me in ways that have deepened and expanded my understanding beyond the scope of traditional religion. I have learned that we all have access to the highest vibrations of Creator's light. Whatever your path, walk it! Investigate it. Don't be afraid to go beyond that which you know as "truth". Remember, people once believed the world was flat!

My hope is that you will find that the beliefs you currently hold, whatever they may be, are accentuated by the precepts held within this book. If you currently identify with a particular spiritual path, I think this book will only serve to deepen your faith. Don't get caught up in religious dogma or semantics. Read it in the spirit in which it is intended. Get to the core message of love!

Essentially, this book examines three main principles:

1) You are both a human and divine being. The primary purpose of your life is to understand and integrate these two seemingly opposing states of 'being' (which I refer to as "The Me I Couldn't See"). By doing so, you begin to find your authentic self.

2) Creator loves you unconditionally. As you learn to receive His love, you begin to trust and surrender to it, learning to love yourself and others in the process.

3) Finding your inner voice of truth and honoring it is the key to living in authenticity. By becoming aware of your truth, you can avoid being tossed around by your own unconscious creation and create the life you really want to live.

I chose to write this book at this specific time because we are at an important phase in the evolution of human consciousness. I've come to realize that the purpose of my life is deeply rooted in the need to balance the masculine and feminine aspects of this three-dimensional world. Much of the trauma in my life has been about this very issue – suppression of the feminine in favor of the masculine and the need to correct this imbalance from within myself, which in turn corrects the imbalance in my external reality. I believe this is the key to creating global and cultural stability for humanity. This important shift is already well underway, and more than likely, if you were called to read this book, you are key player in making this happen.

Of course, the shift for humanity begins inside of you. Be the change you want to see in the world. Are you open to seeing things from a new perspective? Or do you prefer to keep trying to prove the old paradigms right? If this book offers you anything at all, I pray that you uncover your own patterns and that you are courageous enough to look at them honestly. There is no reason to feel guilt or shame about anything because everything in your life up to this point is exactly how it was meant to be. I hope you can ask, "Is this assumption I hold about myself and my life really true for me now?" This book is about weeding out old ways of thinking and operating in the world so that you may transform yourself and your life from the inside out.

This book is also meant to help you realize how much power you really have within you. Everything in your life you have called in through your vibration; the essence of you in spiritual form. It is a part of "The Me I Couldn't See". While circumstances seem to appear on their own, they are really vibrations of ourselves manifest in concrete ways, so we can understand what we are doing. With this realization, however, comes great personal responsibility for our own choices and circumstances. In many ways, it is easier to keep believing that we're the victims of our circumstances and that our lives are beyond our control. I am insisting that the opposite is true and that you are responsible consciously or unconsciously for the interactions with everything and everyone in your life.

Perhaps this idea is hard for you because there is something in your life that you think will never change. Or maybe you just feel stuck and don't know how to move forward in life. This book is meant to challenge you and to push the limits of your beliefs about yourself and the world. Are you willing to look at new possibilities? Is it possible that the Earth and everything in this dimension is only a mirror of illusion, and that the authentic, divine YOU is in a higher dimension? Is it possible that as you listen to the still, small voice within, that you will be able to open new gifts and abilities beyond the five senses?

The first important lesson in this book is that we are ALWAYS loved unconditionally. Only the ego gives you the illusion that you are unloved, unacceptable or not enough for Creator or, contrarily, too good for Creator! As we move beyond the ego of the mind into the space of heart, we are able to accept and love ourselves more fully, and in turn, are able to love others just as they are. Nothing about you or anyone around you needs to be "fixed." You are exactly as you are meant to be at this particular moment in time. Until now, you made the best choices you could in the moment. You are a being who was uniquely conceived by Creator as an expression of Creator. You, like every other human being, have a special role to play as His divine co-creator. It's time for all humanity to move out of the "drift" of the unconscious and into pure love, finding our authentic selves. It's the reason we came here!

Shakespeare is famous for having said, "All the world's a stage and all the men and women are merely players." Indeed, life as most people are currently living it is like a huge masquerade ball. It can be fun for a while, but at some point you might want to take off the mask to live more authentically. Are you ready to drop the costume? If you are ready to ask the bigger questions, you're ready to open and learn and transform into the authentic you. I invite you to come along with me on the journey toward **The Me I Couldn't See.**

EPILOGUE

Where Do We Go From Here?

Wisdom is knowledge applied. Head knowledge is useless on the battlefield. Knowledge stamped on the heart makes one wise.

- Beth Moore

I have set out to achieve some pretty big things with this book. Let's take inventory of where we are by contemplating some important questions:

- How am I feeling about myself? Do I feel whole, perfect and complete?
- Have I become more aware of where I am standing in relationship to life?
- Am I consciously aware of what I am creating, or am I letting circumstances control me?
- Am I aware of my own duality? (both human and divine?)
- Am I ready to be self-honest before my Creator?
- Am I a victim of life or a Master of it?

- Am I taking responsibility for everything outside of me, knowing that it is simply the manifestation of what is actually happening within me?
- Am I recognizing when I am in my ego (mind) and when I am in my higher heart? (Spirit)
- Am I choosing minute by minute what I want in life?
- Am I willing to look at balance in all things?
- Can I hear my inner voice? How do I know it's not my ego?
- Am I a perpetual learner, open to new ways of perceiving things?
- Am I growing, or am I stagnating?

Assessment and contemplation are necessary for growth. The work is worth it!

We are not victims. In fact, we are co-creators with Divine Source! We are completely loved and worthy. <u>Begin to live the truth of who you are</u>. It takes guts! Face your dark or shadow side. Own it. Love it, so it can be disempowered. Meditate. Pray. Enjoy life. Don't get caught up in other peoples' opinions and laws. Be OUTSTANDING and jump into the depths of the creativity of your Spirit and into the unknown. That's where the magic is… and where you will reunite with THE ME I COULDN'T SEE!